Janet Morley is a freelance v
She has worked for Christian Aid and for the Methodist Church,
and is the author of several books of prayers and poems, including
All Desires Known and *Bread of Tomorrow*, both published by SPCK.

THE HEART'S TIME

A poem a day for Lent and Easter

Janet Morley

First published in Great Britain in 2011

Society for Promoting Christian Knowledge
36 Causton Street
London SW1P 4ST
www.spckpublishing.co.uk

British Library Cataloguing-in-Publication Data
A catalogue record for this book is available from the British Library

ISBN 978–0–281–06372–7

Typeset by Caroline Waldron, Wirral, Cheshire
Printed in Great Britain by Ashford Colour Press
Subsequently digitally printed in Great Britain

Produced on paper from sustainable forests

Contents

Introduction   ix

'Turning aside to the miracle' – Engaging with Lent

Ash Wednesday	The Bright Field	R. S. Thomas	3
Thursday	Trinity Sunday	George Herbert	6
Friday	Lent	Jean M. Watt	8
Saturday	On a Theme by Thomas Merton	Denise Levertov	10

Week 1
'What country do we come from?' – Expressing our longings

Monday	Homesick	Carol Ann Duffy	15
Tuesday	Beauty so ancient and so new	Augustine	18
Wednesday	Before I got my eye put out	Emily Dickinson	21
Thursday	The Call	Charlotte Mew	24
Friday	I Saw him Standing	Ann Griffiths	27
Saturday	Speaking in tongues	Kei Miller	30

Week 2
'How can it need so agonized an effort?' – Struggle

Monday	Alas my Lord	Christina Rossetti	35
Tuesday	Affliction	George Herbert	39
Wednesday	It is dangerous to read newspapers	Margaret Atwood	42
Thursday	A Poison Tree	William Blake	45

Contents

| Friday | Thou art indeed just | Gerard Manley Hopkins | 48 |
| Saturday | The Wrong Beds | Roger McGough | 51 |

Week 3
'At home in the house of the living' – Being where we are

Monday	Pax	D. H. Lawrence	57
Tuesday	Friends' Meeting House, Frenchay, Bristol	U. A. Fanthorpe	60
Wednesday	i am a little church	E. E. Cummings	63
Thursday	The Moment	Margaret Atwood	66
Friday	Rembrandt's Late Self-Portraits	Elizabeth Jennings	69
Saturday	The Trees	Philip Larkin	72

Week 4
'A reckless way of going' – Facing suffering and death

Monday	Epitaph	Sir Walter Ralegh	77
Tuesday	The Soul's Garment	Margaret Cavendish	80
Wednesday	Because I could not stop for Death	Emily Dickinson	82
Thursday	Deaths of Flowers	E. J. Scovell	85
Friday	On his blindness	John Milton	88
Saturday	The problem	Adrienne Rich	91

Week 5
'There are quite different things going on' – Altered perspectives

Monday	The Kingdom	R. S. Thomas	97
Tuesday	The Skylight	Seamus Heaney	100
Wednesday	Rublev	Rowan Williams	103
Thursday	Sheep Fair Day	Kerry Hardie	107
Friday	Afterwards	U. A. Fanthorpe	111
Saturday	The Donkey	G. K. Chesterton	114

Contents

Week 6
'Love's austere and lonely offices' – Holy Week

Monday	Those Winter Sundays	Robert Hayden	119
Tuesday	Fire and Ice	Robert Frost	122
Wednesday	I am the great sun	Charles Causley	124
Maundy Thursday	Love	George Herbert	128
Good Friday	Good Friday, 1613. Riding Westward	John Donne	131
Holy Saturday	Ikon: The Harrowing of Hell	Denise Levertov	135

Week 7
'Never turning away again' – Resurrection

Easter Monday	i thank You God	E. E. Cummings	141
Tuesday	Food for risen bodies – II	Michael Symmons Roberts	144
Wednesday	The Angel	Ruth Fainlight	147
Thursday	Resurrection	R. S. Thomas	150
Friday	A Birthday	Christina Rossetti	153
Saturday	And that will be heaven	Evangeline Paterson	156

Acknowledgements	159

Introduction

Poetry and the spiritual life

'To know a poem
by heart
is to slow down
to the heart's time.'

Nicholas Albery

Reading poetry offers a distinctive resource for our spiritual life; and this is true of a wide variety of poems. Some, but by no means all, of the poems in this book have been written with a consciously religious intention. Others have not, but have been selected because they are addressing, in a truthful and productive way, matters that Christians can helpfully reflect on. Their brief and vivid form makes poems infinitely *usable*. And the very process of engaging with poetry is valuable in the spiritual journey.

- Poetry makes us slow down. It is spare writing, where each word, its rhythm and place in the text, works hard to convey layers of meaning. Often the reader needs to speak the poem out loud. Slow reading is particularly helpful in a society where, increasingly, our electronic communications encourage us to skim read, accept interruption to our concentration, and generally do several things at once rather than ever go deep. Though poetry is brief, it can open up our contemplative focus.
- Poetry is thought of as classically dealing in joy and passion, and the beauties of the natural world – and so it does, in vivid and moving detail. But poets are also among the few in our society

who explore hard subjects head on: ageing, pain, loneliness, the failing of the memory and the inevitability of death. Poetry helps us face the realities of the human condition.

- In joy and in pain, people need and cling to patterned words. Even those who do not normally read poetry or attend worship find meaning and comfort in familiar words that put things succinctly or are linked to ritual that speaks of a path that others have shared.

- Liturgical words, prayers and songs that are used in public worship must address the whole story of salvation and must avoid irony, doubt, humour, and idiosyncratic perspectives. But poetry can engage with all of these things, which makes it a particular resource for personal exploration. And it is free to be partial – to investigate just one part of the truth.

- So concentration on detail is a distinctive strength of poetry. Poets pick out aspects of reality (inner and outer) that may otherwise have gone unnoticed; yet when highlighted bring recognition and insight. Ruth Padel speaks of her sceptical scientist mother who, when eventually dragged to a poetry reading, admitted, 'I see the point of poets now. They *notice* things.' Spiritual insight arises from accurate observation, rather than soft-focusing.

- But poetry leaves a good deal of room for the reader to appreciate different layers of meaning. Tennyson remarked that poetry is like 'shot silk with many glancing colours' in which each reader finds their own interpretation. The reader needs to work at finding the meaning, and cannot just read it off from someone else's commentary or settle on a certainty. Reading poetry demands that the intelligence works hard, but in the service of the heart.

- The images evoked by a poem, the sounds of its words, and phrases that feel especially salient can linger in the mind like a remembered melody. The poem can stay with us during the day or return much later, bringing new insight as we ourselves mature in spiritual understanding.

- It is common for a poem to examine something familiar in such a way that it becomes newly strange. Applied to religious truth, this denies us the comfort of taking refuge in formulae. Poetry helps us in the process of 'unlearning', which is a necessary part of the spiritual journey.

- Many Christian writers have found that writing poetry is a profound way to engage in prayer or to reflect on the nature of prayer (for instance, George Herbert, R. S. Thomas). Others who do not fully inhabit the Christian tradition have seen parallels between trying to write poetry and trying to pray. Kei Miller's 'Speaking in tongues' (pp. 30–1) proposes that 'each poem is waiting on its own Day of Pentecost', seeking to be open to the divine spirit, to the language of God, the miracle of being understood.

- For many poets (not only the intentionally Christian writers), the language and stories of the Bible, and the myriad ways it has been interpreted, have become part of the cultural and psychic background from which they write. Sometimes they explicitly and intriguingly retell or reference biblical texts, but often there are subtler references, which may need highlighting in order to access some of the layers of meaning in a poem. This can then throw new light on our inherited traditions.

So poetry offers us a way of being truly experimental in our spiritual life. It gives us a chance to address God more boldly, to test out our beliefs, to examine our vocation, to acknowledge our capacity for self-delusion and to give voice to our deepest longings.

The poems and the themes of Lent

Lent is a period of the year when Christians set aside time to reflect on their spiritual journey; it is appropriately 'the heart's time'. The book is organized into a series of weekly themes, offering a poem a day for Monday to Saturday, from Ash Wednesday to the Saturday after Easter.

'Turning aside to the miracle' – Engaging with Lent

The first four poems have been chosen to introduce Lent as a time of focus and concentration, of stopping to *notice* what matters most in life. We turn aside to receive the blessing of the present moment;

we name our intention to turn to God; we consent to be stripped of what distracts us; we are truthful about the deceptive pleasures that mesmerize us and prevent us from being aware of God's surrounding love.

'What country do we come from?' – Expressing our longings

In the first full week of Lent, the poems are about what we seriously desire and long for. We need to try to articulate these in order to refocus our lives and the actual priorities we are living by. Yet by their nature, our deepest longings are very difficult to explain, and the explanations will leave more unsaid than precisely said. These poems are about 'homesickness'; about unsatisfied passion; a new way of seeing the world; a sense of call that leaves us no way back; a vision of beauty, not quite available; or, even, an experience of sheer embarrassment that nevertheless speaks of the meaning of our lives.

'How can it need so agonized an effort?' – Struggle

Those who seriously seek to engage with the Christian life will soon discover that quite a lot of struggle is involved, as prayer proves difficult, boring, or apparently barren, and growing self-knowledge can give way to a debilitating despair. We wrestle with our involvement in the violence of the world, the shocking force of our own hatreds, and the disappointments life brings even to those who have dedicated their lives to God's service. These are poems that look steadily, sometimes humorously, at our self-delusions and unlovely motivations.

'At home in the house of the living' – Being where we are

In this section, the poems have been chosen to explore self-examination that is both truthful and accepting of ourselves and our place in the world. There is an emphasis on a more peaceful approach to prayer, with attentive stillness at its centre, waiting on the presence of God. The point is to inhabit where we are in the created world, without seeking to possess it. We are invited to become more fully self-aware; this is where 'all the darknesses are dared', but hope is possible.

'A reckless way of going' – Facing suffering and death

Contemplating our mortality is a traditional Lenten practice which is not popular these days; but since it is the fundamental condition we live with, there is relief and blessing in facing it. Here are several poems that explore the prospect and meaning of death, but in different ways that reflect the century they were written in. Reflecting on death has an impact on how we choose then to live, and make priorities. The last two poems in this section explore the insights about the world or our vocation in it that emerge from living with disability, pain or other constraints.

'There are quite different things going on' – Altered perspectives

Poetry's ability to concentrate on small things makes it a powerful tool for examining life from the underside; and this can reflect the Christian understanding of the 'kingdom of God', the main theme of Jesus' teaching in the Gospels. In these poems, unusual perspectives are adopted, which ask us to look at the world and its understanding about power from an unexpected angle. Familiar or ordinary things – a theatrical play, an icon, a day at the cattle market, a well-known Gospel story – are made strange again and new insight becomes available.

'Love's austere and lonely offices' – Holy Week

The poems for Holy Week explore some of the depths of human hatred and betrayal, as well as God's pain at suffering our rejection. Yet at the heart of this week is the offer of love even at the point of greatest evil, even when we are reluctant to accept forgiveness and refreshment. Reluctant as we are to look at the cross, God asks us even there to turn our face and be received again. The week ends with a longer poem which starts with the 'harrowing of hell', but becomes a profound and moving process of revisiting the meaning and experience of incarnation.

'Never turning away again' – Resurrection

The poems continue into the week after Easter, and they reflect something of the variety of reactions to the resurrection that is found in the Gospel narratives. There is great joy and amazement, but also a sense of confusion. Some of the poems retell or reflect on Gospel stories, and some explore what resurrection means now: in the world and in our hearts.

Ways of using this book

The book is written mainly for individuals to read during Lent, taking one poem a day to reflect on slowly, perhaps choosing to learn the poem by heart. It may help to have a Bible to hand as well. My commentary tries to pick out and briefly explain the major biblical resonances in a poem: the reader may well find more, that I have missed. The commentaries are my reading of the poems, intended to provoke thought, not to be the last word on the subject.

The Heart's Time can also be used with a weekly group, which might:

- agree to read the poems selected each week;
- have each person choose one or two that were most helpful (or puzzling), and say why, then read the poem aloud;
- allow discussion to arise from the choices people make – and compare or contrast poems with those previously discussed;
- have a time of silence and prayer that emerges from the group's discussion of the poems.

A group that benefits from reading poetry and sharing reflection on it may wish to continue beyond Lent with its own choice of poems.

'Turning aside to the miracle'
Engaging with Lent

Ash Wednesday

The Bright Field

I have seen the sun break through
to illuminate a small field
for a while, and gone my way
and forgotten it. But that was the pearl
of great price, the one field that had
the treasure in it. I realize now
that I must give all that I have
to possess it. Life is not hurrying

on to a receding future, nor hankering after
an imagined past. It is the turning
aside like Moses to the miracle
of the lit bush, to a brightness
that seemed as transitory as your youth
once, but is the eternity that awaits you.

R. S. Thomas

To keep Lent is to turn aside from the ordinary routines of our life in order to reflect; to notice what is going on, to detect what is really significant. It is to attend properly to what seems insignificant and might otherwise be missed, but is actually indicative of the whole direction of our unconscious priorities – so that these can be reconsidered. It is consciously to take a slice out of ordinary time, so as to understand how we use time overall.

This deceptively simple, almost conversational poem uses the classic form of a Petrarchan sonnet (eight lines to propose an idea – the octet – then a 'turn' into the six lines – the sestet – that develop this idea and resolve it or take it in a new direction). The poet is describing the common rural experience of observing how a particular kind of weather – clouds and sunny intervals – can fleetingly have the effect of highlighting one particular field in a landscape, as if picking it out deliberately. He puts this contemporary and commonplace experience alongside two biblical passages: the story of Moses turning aside to the burning bush (Exodus 3), and the two brief parables Jesus told about a pearl of great price and a field with buried treasure in it (Matthew 13.44–45). These required their purchasers to sacrifice everything else they had in order to buy them.

The temporarily sunlit field, which the poet observed and then forgot, becomes an image of 'the one field that had/ the treasure in it' – the opportunity to see and then make a sacrificial but deeply rewarding choice of direction in life. Notice the double meaning on 'break through'. As the poem moves into the sestet, the bright field merges with the image of the 'lit bush' which Moses turns aside to see, which reveals the voice of God and begins the story of the liberation of a community from slavery. Both the field and the bush are ordinary features of landscape that are temporarily lit up with transcendence. A life-changing encounter with the holy is possible – so long as we will turn aside and take notice.

The two parts of the sonnet are linked by a remark about the nature of human life and how we go through it. This is highlighted by its place as the hinge of the poem, insisting as it does on pressing onwards rather than letting the reader take a breath at the end of the first eight lines. And here the poet does some strange things with our expectations about past and future, and how we relate to time.

The normal cliché is that we hanker after an imagined future, and that it is the past that recedes, but the poet's reversal of these terms pushes us to look freshly at what in fact we do. 'Hurrying on' is what we do when we will not stop and notice the present moment with its bright blessing. Yet we do not ever reach the future we move towards – it recedes as each moment becomes that present in which, once again, we may choose to take notice of (or miss) the open opportunity. And the past, on the face of it something we should be able to remember, tends to become a closed, selective confection about which we can feel nostalgic – 'hankering' for its imagined simplicity.

The poet returns to the image of brightness, and again confuses expectations – it 'seemed as transitory as your youth/ once'. The observation that youth is transitory, like the momentary highlighting of a sunlit field, is a middle-aged perception. (When actually young, the impression is that youth will last indefinitely.) But the poet is pushing beyond the cynicism and disappointment of middle age to assert that to see the fleeting illumination which occurs in the present moment is also to perceive 'the eternity that awaits you' – not a receding, ever inaccessible future, but a profound reality that calmly waits to embrace our preoccupied, harassed selves, if only we will stop properly, and look, and choose.

What has prompted you to choose to 'turn aside' this Lent?

Thursday

Trinity Sunday

Lord, who hast form'd me out of mud,
    And hast redeem'd me through thy blood,
    And sanctified me to do good;

Purge all my sins done heretofore;
    For I confess my heavy score,
    And I will strive to sin no more.

Enrich my heart, mouth, hands in me,
    With faith, with hope, with charity;
    That I may run, rise, rest with thee.

George Herbert

It may seem strange to choose a poem called 'Trinity Sunday' to reflect on at the start of Lent, but in fact the themes of this poem-prayer are central to the traditional observance of the Lenten season. The poem's narrator recalls his place in the story of creation and salvation, offers confession for sin, and dedicates himself to a life lived more closely with God. Thus the poem implicitly invites readers to place themselves in this story and respond in the same way.

The first line of the poem takes us back to the traditional words used on Ash Wednesday when an ash cross is inscribed on the worshipper's forehead: 'Remember that you are dust, and to dust you shall return.' This itself recalls the story of the creation of human beings in Genesis 2, where God creates Adam from the dust of the earth, and then, after the Fall, announces with this phrase the certainty of human death and return to the dust. It is echoed again in the funeral service: 'earth to earth, ashes to ashes, dust to dust'. Thus, those who are receiving the mark of the cross in dust and ashes are thereby recognizing with humility that they are God's earthbound creatures; that they are complicit in a sinful and disordered world; and that they are mortal and will die. On the face of it a ritual that could be gloomy and self-abasing, it can be a refreshing reality check. These are indeed the terms in which we live our lives before God.

In this poem the tone is completely straightforward, and indeed in his choice of words the poet lifts us straight from the dry dust of the Middle East, where the creation story emerged, to the damp heaviness of the earth in an English rural landscape: 'Lord, who hast form'd me out of mud'. With such a homely, almost childish word he rhymes the redeeming 'blood' of Christ, and the effect is to bring redemption into the intimate realm of the ordinary, contemporary world. The process of sanctification, likewise, is the simple desire to 'do good'.

The second stanza, which moves from the context of salvation's story to the confession of sin, represents the intention of the narrator to place himself within the story and to repent accordingly. Given the fondness of many writers of Herbert's time to dwell on their sins, sometimes in luxuriously tortured detail, there is something powerful about the spare reference simply to a 'heavy score' and to the commitment to 'strive to sin no more'. The poem operates here in the same way that good liturgy does, offering a container which the reader's or worshipper's reality can invest with personal meaning.

The final stanza moves swiftly from the acknowledgement of sin to the grasping of hope for an enriched life with God. Here the insistent 'threeness' motif of a poem to the Trinity (three stanzas of three lines each) comes to a head: the poet's immediate lived life – feelings, speech and action ('heart, mouth, hands') – are linked with the three cardinal virtues (faith, hope, charity) so that he may 'run, rise, rest' with God. The final three words have double meanings: they are both about the dailiness of actions like getting up, going about and going to sleep, and about the whole of life and what follows after death: running life's course as a mortal being, rising at the general resurrection of the dead, and resting with God in eternity.

Try using this poem as your own prayer. You may want to memorize it.

Friday

---·•·---

Lent

Lent is a tree without blossom, without leaf,
Barer than blackthorn in its winter sleep,
All unadorned. Unlike Christmas which decrees
The setting-up, the dressing-up of trees,
Lent is a taking down, a stripping bare,
A starkness after all has been withdrawn
Of surplus and superfluous,
Leaving no hiding-place, only an emptiness
Between black branches, a most precious space
Before the leaf, before the time of flowers;
Lest we should see only the leaf, the flower,
Lest we should miss the stars.

Jean M. Watt

In the northern hemisphere, our experience of Lent and its traditional practices is strongly linked with what is normally happening
in terms of the weather and the progression of the seasons. Unless
Easter is very late, or spring exceptionally early, the start of Lent falls
at a time that is still cold and wintry, before most of the buds and
shoots have even begun to stir. However, at Easter, spring is definitely
coming and the first flowers of the year are blooming and leaves are
emerging as if to greet the resurrection. Many poets mine the season
of spring for metaphors of the spiritual life.

This poem, interestingly, celebrates that cold space at the start of
Lent, when trees and bushes are still bare and unadorned, and links

this to the practice of abstinence, of stripping down to the basics. Although it speaks of a time that is cold and exposed, the mood is not gloomy – there is even a certain gentleness about the 'blackthorn in its winter sleep'. (Blackthorn is the first tree to flower, and the white flowers come before the leaves do, so that its first snowy blossoms are sometimes called a 'blackthorn winter'.) The poem contrasts this time of 'stripping bare' with the Christmas festival, which ordains that trees shall be set up and dressed extravagantly. Many find that there is a certain austere pleasure in clearing up after the excesses of Christmas, and taking on the disciplines of Lent, giving up the 'surplus and superfluous'.

The second half of the poem explores what is at the heart of doing without decoration. It is both challenging and inspiring. There is 'no hiding-place', but the emptiness is a 'most precious space' that deserves to be noticed in its own right. I was expecting the poem to highlight the elegant, essential structure of the branches and shape of trees that can only be seen before the leaves and blossom emerge. But the last line mentions instead what can only be seen when the branches are bare – the distant stars now caught in the twigs, which will be hidden from view and eclipsed when the leaves are thick and the blossom flaunting itself.

Suddenly the whole perspective of the poem has shifted from close inspection of blackthorn hedges and Christmas trees to the vastness of the universe. In the same way, we are invited to allow the intentional keeping of Lent to rearrange our habitual perspectives on life, to let ourselves be unsettled so that we do not miss God's wider vision.

Is there anything you find you enjoy about Lent?

Saturday

—•—

On a Theme by Thomas Merton

'Adam, where are you?'
       God's hands
palpate darkness, the void
that is Adam's inattention,
his confused attention to everything,
impassioned by multiplicity, his despair.

  Multiplicity, his despair;
       God's hands
enacting blindness. Like a child
at a barbaric fairground –
noise, lights, the violent odors –
Adam fragments himself. The whirling rides!

  Fragmented Adam stares.
       God's hands
unseen, the whirling rides
dazzle, the lights blind him. Fragmented,
he is not present to himself. God
suffers the void that is his absence.

Denise Levertov

In this poem we return both to the story of creation and to the problem of our human inattention to what is most important. The poem explores the nature of humanity's fallen condition, and the effect of that on God's relationship with us – what does it feel like to be 'fallen'? What goes wrong with that vital relationship?

The poem begins with God's question in the garden of Eden after the fruit has been eaten and Adam and Eve have hidden themselves from the presence of God. In the biblical story the question precedes a scene of confession and judgement, but in this poem it seems to characterize a tender God who is helpless to reach his beloved human creature, and whose loving hands try, without success, to touch and call Adam back. It is God, rather than a condemned human being, who suffers the void in the relationship.

Meanwhile, Adam's attention is mesmerized elsewhere, like a child who is bewitched and overwhelmed by the multifarious attractions of a funfair. Fallenness is depicted as the splitting and fragmenting of attention away from the truly significant and in the direction of countless stimulating distractions. Inattention to God is expressed as a confused attention to everything else on the horizon simultaneously. He is 'impassioned' not by love of God but 'multiplicity'. Inattention to God means that the human creature is also 'not present to himself'. This is the same thing as despair. For the image of the funfair and the child, which sounds potentially both fun and innocent, in fact resonates with danger. It is 'barbaric'; the odours are 'violent'; the 'whirling rides' dazzle – and not, it is implied, in a good way.

The poem is very deliberately structured, with a series of repetitions that have contrasting effects. In each stanza, 'God's hands', unseen by Adam, are highlighted to the reader by their position standing alone in the second line, as if underpinning or trying to protect the situation suggested by the first line. Meanwhile, key phrases thrown up at the end of one stanza are reintroduced at the beginning of the next: 'multiplicity, his despair'; 'Adam fragments himself. The whirling rides!/ Fragmented Adam'. Thus the poem itself whirls and circles like the rides, and the jagged repeating phrases echo the fragmentation that is the poem's subject. Meanwhile, in contrast with the mesmerized staring that induces Adam's muddled consciousness, the activity of God is tactile, palpating (as the hands of a healer might) the dark void that exists between creator and creature.

Our contemporary culture is characterized by ceaseless visual and verbal stimulation: news, commentary, entertainment, promotions and adverts, email, online social networking, mobile phones. It is normal now to combine activities simultaneously such as phoning and shopping, studying and listening to music, even dealing with emails or texts while sitting in a meeting. The variety of means of communication has made multitasking and constant interruption of focus part of the texture of everyday life – however, it is never actually possible to 'keep up'. Recent research suggests that the human brain, while it enjoys new stimulation, is less efficient than we like to believe when it is required to multitask. By contrast, the practice of prayer or silent retreat is likely initially to throw up a sense of lostness and boredom, and an internal cacophony, when external stimuli are absent. Nevertheless it is an essential place to start, when seeking to become conscious of the hands of God.

Consider deliberately 'fasting' from some or all kinds of electronic stimulation of your mind for a particular period of each day during Lent, and reflect on what the experience does to your capacity for focus on what matters most.

WEEK 1

'What country do we come from?'

Expressing our longings

Monday

Homesick

When we love, when we tell ourselves we do,
we are pining for first love, somewhen,
before we thought of wanting it. When we rearrange
the rooms we end up living in, we are looking
for first light, the arrangement of light,
that time, before we knew to call it light.

Or talk of music, when we say
we cannot talk of it, but play again
C major, A flat minor, we are straining
for first sound, what we heard once,
then, in lost chords, wordless languages.

What country do we come from? This one?
The one where the sun burns
when we have night? The one
the moon chills; elsewhere, possible?

Why is our love imperfect,
music only echo of itself,
the light wrong?

We scratch in dust with sticks,
dying of homesickness
for when, where, what.

Carol Ann Duffy

Lent is a time to turn aside and focus on ourselves before God as honestly as we can, and a key part of this self-knowledge is the investigation of what it is that we truly long for. It is to articulate where we belong, whether or not we seem, in our fragmented and preoccupied lives, to be headed in that direction at present. It is to register where, what or who it is that we feel 'homesick' for.

This poem speaks to a sense of feeling profoundly and existentially homesick, but not knowing what we are homesick for. The poet explores aspects of experience (falling in love, rearranging rooms to see how the light falls differently, playing music in major or minor keys) that suggest indescribable primal realities behind them. These are the realities we are searching for when we engage in these activities, but we are unable even to articulate them properly. It is as if we are, our whole lives, in a country that is not really ours, which leaves us literally 'dying of homesickness' before we find out what we are pining for.

The tone of the poem throughout is one of uncertainty, of trying a phrase and then putting it another way, always hesitant to say anything definite about our current existence. 'When we love' is immediately followed by the cautious 'when we tell ourselves we do', which stresses the potential self-deception involved, and the disappointment when love goes wrong. But there is a conviction that the 'first love' we are pining for existed, even though we don't exactly remember it. It was 'somewhen'. Similarly, our current activity in arranging our homes seems very provisional and not quite chosen; we rearrange 'rooms we end up living in'. But somewhere there existed 'first light' – some arrangement of light that felt right, before we had language to describe it. Playing music seems aimless and experimental, in this key or that, 'straining/ for first sound'. There is a conviction that we heard it once, but the chords are lost, and any language that might be used about it is 'wordless'.

The stanza that asks, 'What country do we come from?' becomes increasingly inarticulate and confusing; sun and moon, burning heat and chilliness seem mixed up in a phantasmagoric oddness which is our experience of living human lives. And it leads on to the anguished question at the heart of the poem: 'Why is our love imperfect,/ music only echo of itself,/ the light wrong?' It is a cry demanding to know why human life feels less real than we instinctively know it can or should be.

So what are the indescribable but real 'first love', 'first light', 'first sound' that the poem speaks of? At one level these could be about life in the womb or the first emergence from it into the light: the primal love of the mother, as the totally needy newborn child experiences it; the arrangement of light that was actually there in the birthing chamber; the sound of the mother's heartbeat from inside the womb, or when held in her arms. All these would be prior to conscious memory and prior to language and any knowledge of what to call these things.

But I can't escape the feeling that the poet is asking questions that are much more profound than 'why can't we just return to the comfort of the womb?' Early, pre-linguistic experience undoubtedly has a deep influence on our personality and psyche, and there may be a continuing but futile unconscious wish to return to the paradisal time when we could not distinguish ourselves from our mothers. But the poem suggests that our conviction is a true insight: that there is a 'more real' place that we instinctively know about but do not now inhabit.

It is possible to read the poem as referring to the Platonic Forms of reality that the Greek philosopher believed existed: absolute realities of which the earthly experiences we have are only flickering shadows projected on the wall of a cave. The poet leaves us with no certain clues. Throughout, the poem makes no direct mention of God or any sort of faith (unless the scratching 'in dust with sticks' is an oblique reference to Jesus writing in the dust in John 8.6).

But the malaise conveyed here, that painful sense of life being endlessly less than fully real and fully satisfying, could almost be a meditation on the saying of St Augustine: 'Our hearts are restless until they find their rest in thee.'

Do you recognize the feelings this poem describes?

Tuesday

———◦◦◦———

Late have I loved you, Beauty so ancient and so new,
late have I loved you!
Lo, you were within,
but I outside, seeking there for you,
and upon the shapely things you have made I rushed headlong,
I, misshapen.
You were with me, but I was not with you.
They held me back far from you,
those things which would have no being
were they not in you.
You called, shouted, broke through my deafness;
you flared, blazed, banished my blindness;
you lavished your fragrance, I gasped, and now I pant for you;
I tasted you, and I hunger and thirst;
you touched me, and I burned for your peace.

Augustine, trans. Maria Boulding

Most people are strongly affected by this very famous passage of St Augustine's *Confessions* when they come across it for the first time. It is not exactly a poem, but it is, within a long discursive text, a passionate prayer to God. It is not just about the writer's deepest longings, but it is in the form of a love song to the divinity. There is a strong sense of the seeker who is frantic to find his beloved, and yet somehow attempting the search in all the wrong ways. The God who is always present has to break through the barriers that the seeker is unconsciously erecting against the very reality he is desperate to reach.

The first two lines are arresting, setting the tone of this passage. This is reminiscent of the passionate searching for the beloved that is found in the Song of Songs, a biblical love poem which in the early Christian centuries was a constant wellspring for preaching and spirituality. The language of erotic love, with its energy and sensuousness, matched the sense of overpowering desire for that union with God which is the treasure that it would be worth giving everything to possess. Augustine was an adult convert, hence his sense of coming 'late' to love. But the cry immediately sets up the contrast between the human being – subject to time, late, tardy in reacting – and the divine – beyond time, eternal, both deeply ancient and also fresh.

This contrast continues in the next eight lines. It is as if the seeker, while having God within unknown, ignores and rushes past God, seeking outside himself (cf. the earlier poem, 'On a Theme by Thomas Merton', where Adam 'is not present to himself', p. 10). Feeling misshapen or deformed, he flings himself on the shapely, beautifully formed things of God's creation. It is not that God is not inherent in creation, but because of the alienated state of the seeker ('You were with me, but I was not with you') they hold him back from sensing God's presence.

The final five lines speak of the action of God, which is experienced as quite violently sensuous, almost as if gentleness would not get through. But there are strong biblical resonances. Each of the senses is addressed in turn: hearing ('You called, shouted' – like God to Adam in the garden); sight ('you flared, blazed' – like Moses' burning bush that was not consumed); smell ('you lavished your fragrance' – like the woman who broke the alabaster box of perfume to anoint Jesus, Mark 14.3); taste (as in the psalms, 'O taste and see that the LORD is good', Psalm 34.8); touch ('you touched me, and I burned' as in the Song of Songs and in all the healing miracles where Jesus lays hands on the sick).

The effect of God's 'breaking through' the seeker's self-induced inability to see, hear and receive is not calming. It is as if the finding of God (or rather, the being found by God) itself creates an even stronger desire and longing: 'I pant for you', 'I hunger and thirst', 'I burned for your peace.' This is a longing that is going to consume all that we are.

'Spirituality' is popular in contemporary culture, but it has a certain voluntariness and soft focus that earlier Christian writers would have had difficulty in recognizing as the same impulse as the all-consuming desire that drove them.

In what ways have you experienced God breaking through your defences? Try writing your own 'love letter' to God.

Wednesday

Before I got my eye put out
I liked as well to see –
As other Creatures, that have Eyes
And know no other way –

But were it told to me – Today –
That I might have the sky
For mine – I tell you that my Heart
Would split, for size of me –

The Meadows – mine –
The Mountains – mine –
All Forests – Stintless Stars –
As much of Noon as I could take
Between my finite eyes –

The Motions of the Dipping Birds –
The Morning's Amber Road –
For mine – to look at when I liked –
The News would strike me dead –

So safer – guess – with just my soul
Upon the Window pane –
Where other Creatures put their eyes –
Incautious – of the Sun –

Emily Dickinson

Lent is about seeing things in a different perspective, or taking time to notice what we often pass over. Several of the earlier poems have explored themes of seeing and not seeing (or not seeing properly, or seeing and then forgetting). This one tackles the subject in a way that is characteristically, for Emily Dickinson, arresting, baffling and richly suggestive.

It begins with a stanza that has a deceptively casual and conversational style, almost as if the author were discussing a minor preference she no longer entertains, rather than what is apparently a violent experience of being blinded. And yet there is an immediate implication that having no functioning eyes is in some ways a privileged state, enabling a kind of perception that ordinary people are unaware of – they 'know no other way'.

In the rest of the poem, the assertion seems to be made that the blind narrator feels that if it were granted to her to look upon the sky, the landscape, the activities of the natural world, and the light of the sun, she would find it completely unbearable – her heart 'Would split'; even the news that she would be able to see these things would strike her dead. Much better (or at least 'safer') is to fasten just her soul 'Upon the Window pane'.

What is going on in this curious poem? This surface reading of what it says will not do. There is a passion in the description of the natural world that is completely at odds with this apparent statement of resignation that the narrator will not see these things with her physical eyes and that this does not matter.

Although it is not helpful to assume that the narrator of the poem is the same as the poet herself, there clearly was something wrong with Emily Dickinson's eyes. She was an intensely private person and no certain diagnosis survives. In 1864–65 she spent nearly two years in Boston (away from her home) in treatment under a leading ophthalmologist. Lyndall Gordon (in *Lives like Loaded Guns*, Virago, 2010) suggests that the problem could have been linked to epilepsy, which itself may have given rise to Emily's reclusive way of life. This could have prompted a poem that reflects on the experience of the 'blind seer'. Epileptic seizures – if that is what she experienced – can be preceded by auras that distort visual perception in dramatic and unstable ways.

I think we are alerted as readers by the curious disjuncture between subject matter and tone that something profound and symbolic is intended by the phrase 'Before I got my eye put out'. The poet is signalling a shift in perception that makes previous ways of seeing impossible to sustain, and ultimately neither as truthful nor as satisfying as what the poem's narrator currently experiences.

Although Dickinson does not explicitly reference the Bible, I believe that underlying this poem is a common biblical theme about seeing and not seeing, about human eyes being 'held' until some divine providence causes scales to drop, and about the conviction that to look upon the face of God is to risk immediate death. Several figures in the Old Testament who have experience of the presence of God comment that they have seen God and yet remain alive, as if this can by no means be taken for granted (for example, Hagar in Genesis 16.13, Jacob in Genesis 32.30). When Moses asks to see the face of God, it is said that he would not be able to bear this, so he is hidden in the cleft of a rock and is protected so that he can only glimpse God's retreating back view (Exodus 33.17–23). The poem's reference to 'As much of Noon as I could take/ Between my finite eyes' echoes this idea.

Thus the works of nature, which are so often romanticized – meadows, mountains, forests, stars – become instinct with the sheer intoxicating danger of divine presence.

So, the poem apparently contrasts a blind, reclusive, resigned poet with ordinary creatures who do see the beauties of the natural world. But I believe that it really contrasts the contemplative who is able to apprehend the beauty and terrifying power of God through the divine immanence in the created world, with a way of seeing that has eyes but misses all this, 'Incautious – of the Sun'.

Does contemplative prayer ever seem 'dangerous' to you?

Thursday

The Call

From our low seat beside the fire
    Where we have dozed and dreamed and watched the glow
  Or raked the ashes, stopping so
We scarcely saw the sun or rain
  Above, or looked much higher
Than this same quiet red or burned-out fire.
      To-night we heard a call,
      A rattle on the window-pane,
      A voice on the sharp air,
And felt a breath stirring our hair,
  A flame within us: Something swift and tall
  Swept in and out and that was all.
Was it a bright or a dark angel? Who can know?
  It left no mark upon the snow,
    But suddenly it snapped the chain
    Unbarred, flung wide the door
    Which will not shut again;
  And so we cannot sit here any more.
      We must arise and go:
     The world is cold without
     And dark and hedged about
    With mystery and enmity and doubt,
      But we must go
    Though yet we do not know
Who called, or what marks we shall leave upon the snow.

Charlotte Mew

To keep Lent is to be deliberately reflective, but not to be passive. It is to anticipate the need for significant change in our lives, to be attentive to the possibility of being called into something new.

This poem is about the experience of receiving a call. It works through a single extended image, starting with a cosy but rather lifeless indoor scene by the fireside, which is interrupted by a brisk but mysterious visitor who flings the door open so that it will not shut again. Those inside feel that they have no choice but to go out into the snow themselves – perhaps to discover who the visitor was, but certainly without knowing exactly where they are headed.

The inward-looking, lazy opening scene sets out the lack of direction and the low expectations of whoever is meant by 'we' in the poem. The seat is low, the fire has sunk almost to embers: it is quiet, red, and burned-out. Unlike the unconsumed burning bush of Moses' vision, it is an image of low energy, fatigued faith, absence of passion. The long-vowelled past tenses of the verbs used: 'dozed', 'dreamed', 'watched', 'raked' – all about passivity or languid activity – emphasize decline, slowness, the sense of an ending. The indoor life is about not raising our faces higher than the hearth; the sun and rain outside are barely part of our awareness.

Then there is the sudden hearing of a call, and this is highlighted by the indented lines and the short, brittle word sounds: 'rattle', 'sharp'. Simultaneously, there is a sense of action occurring both outside and inside. First there is something of outdoors that impinges on the room – the call, the rattle, the voice, the breath of air. Then there is a sense of inner response – 'A flame within us'. Unlike the dying fire, which hasn't stirred into flame even with being raked, something inside us has taken fire.

The description of the mysterious visitor is done with speed and brevity, so that what is conveyed is that the visitation happened so fleetingly that it was impossible to remember clearly: 'Something swift and tall/ Swept in and out and that was all'. The alliteration of 'swift' and 'swept' gives the impression of authoritative presence that cannot be captured or held. It is even hard to be sure whether the presence was benign or not, or where indeed it came from: 'It left no mark upon the snow'. Nevertheless, something decisive and exposing has irrevocably happened, even if we don't know what it was. The door chain is 'snapped', the door 'flung wide'. This is an image of something being changed within our psyche and our will, in a way that cannot be denied, and which precludes going back or recreating the original comfortable but dozy fireside scene: 'we cannot sit here any more.'

It is clear, from this enigmatic call, that we have to step out into the cold and dark world beyond the fireside. There is mystery about the call, and more mystery ahead of us. Unlike the angel, we will leave marks on the snow, but as yet their direction, and our impact on the world, is unseen and impossible to describe. There will be doubt and hostility to face. But there is now a conviction that we must follow the call, and 'unknowing' is just part of the deal.

Many would recognize the description of an experience of vocation evoked by this poem. In contrast to some of the biblical stories of encountering angels or the voice of God, there is very little explanation of what is expected. But the sense of compulsion, of being lifted out of our limited horizons, and of the impossibility of going back, are all powerfully present.

Have you ever experienced a sense of calling? What have you done about it?

Friday

I Saw him Standing

Under the dark trees, there he stands,
there he stands; shall he not draw my eyes?
I thought I knew a little
how he compels, beyond all things, but now
he stands there in the shadows. It will be
Oh, such a daybreak, such bright morning,
when I shall wake to see him
as he is.

He is called Rose of Sharon, for his skin
is clear, his skin is flushed with blood,
his body lovely and exact; how he compels
beyond ten thousand rivals. There he stands,
my friend, the friend of guilt and helplessness,
to steer my hollow body
over the sea.

The earth is full of masks and fetishes,
what is there here for me? are these like him?
Keep company with him and you will know:
no kin, no likeness to those empty eyes.
He is a stranger to them all, great Jesus.
What is there here for me? I know
what I have longed for. Him to hold
me always.

Ann Griffiths, trans. Rowan Williams

The rural Welsh poet Ann Griffiths, writing at the end of the eighteenth century, was a young woman who was deeply affected by the Welsh Methodist revival. Initially scornful of the Methodist movement (in her lifetime still part of the established church), she found herself moved and convinced by its teaching – some of which took place in open-air sermons. Alongside the primacy of the Bible, Methodism stressed the importance of spiritual experience in the heart of the believer, and Ann was regarded, even in a time of strong religious awakening, as someone whose experience of God was particularly powerful. Her work combines the sense of conviction of sin with a belief in the utter centrality of Jesus as the beloved Saviour whom she will one day meet and know face to face.

This poem, which uses a range of biblical references, conveys this intensity of longing in language and imagery that is almost startling to the modern reader, because of its erotic charge. However, as we have seen with the passage from St Augustine's *Confessions* (see pp. 18–19), this way of describing the longing of the soul for God is deeply traditional, taking its starting point from the Song of Songs. The poem calls up the image of Jesus as a young man, the poet's beloved, initially seen only in the distance, under the trees and in the shadows. Then his compelling beauty is described in graphic terms and he is claimed as 'my friend'. Finally the intense fleshly beauty of the Saviour is contrasted with the emptiness and falsity of the 'masks' the earth offers us instead. Griffiths' Jesus is eternally a 'stranger' to these things, and his embrace is longed for as the true and eternal reality.

The first stanza could almost be situated in a local forest, the figure under the dark trees an ordinary lover. The narrator's 'double-take' ('I thought I knew a little/ how he compels') beautifully describes the common experience of one in love when meeting the beloved again – the reality is even more heart-stopping than memory imagined. However, it is as if the lover is consciously holding back so as not to be seen quite clearly. This is reminiscent of the Song of Songs chapter 5, which features a passionate woman whose lover seems to come very close and then withdraws, leaving her to search and call for him through the night. The narrator then longs for the 'daybreak', the 'bright morning' when the lover will be seen properly. There may be a reference here to the resurrection narratives (especially Mary Magdalene who in John 20.16 gradually realizes that she has met the risen Christ in the garden), and to St Paul's great hymn to love in 1 Corinthians 13: 'For now we see in a mirror, dimly, but then we will see face to face' (13.12).

The second stanza makes the reference to the Song of Songs explicit, for the Bridegroom is there described as a rose of Sharon (Song of Songs 2.1). It is also said, 'My beloved is all radiant and ruddy, distinguished among ten thousand' (5.10). Since Jesus is also known as David's son, there may be a reference to the anointing of the young David, who stood out among his brothers as 'ruddy' and handsome. But the poet intensifies the biblical image by the physical details that attract: 'his skin is flushed with blood,/ his body lovely and exact'. This is as if a passionate young woman is describing the body of her beloved, which moves her with unashamed erotic power. This highly fleshly figure is the friend of sinners – there is nothing remotely bloodless about this Christ.

By contrast, what the earth offers is 'masks and fetishes' – cold creations that hide or deceive, that cover what is real, or that induce addiction to what is peripheral to reality. There could not be a stronger contrast between the masks and the 'empty eyes' and the face of Christ flushed with blood, exact and compelling. The narrator of this poem is certain what she longs for; it is the touch and embrace of such a Christ, and she is not afraid to describe these in the most intimate terms – 'Him to hold/ me always.'

What do you identify as the 'masks and fetishes' of our contemporary society? How far are you yourself attracted to some of them?

Saturday

———•◆•———

Speaking in tongues

This poem begins in 1987.
My grandmother dragged us to meet the Lord
under a tent in St Catherine. From here
I trace the heritage of standing spellbound
as women worship. Always I am on the outskirts.
I remember my grandmother unbecoming
the kind of woman who sets her table each Sunday,
who walks up from the river, water balanced easily
on her head. My grandmother became, instead,
all earthquake – tilt and twirl and spin,
her orchid-purple skirt blossoming.
She became grunt and rumble – sounds
you can only make when your shoes have fallen off
and you're on the ground
crying *raba* and *yashundai, robosei* and
babababababababba. Years later a friend tells me
tongues is nothing but gibberish – the deluded
pulling words out of dust. I want to ask him
what is language but a sound we christen?
I would invite him to a tent where women
are tearing their stockings, are on the ground
pulling up fresh words to offer as doves to Jehovah.
I would ask him if he sees no meaning here
and if he never had the urge to grunt
an entirely new sound. The poem, always,
would like to do this, always wants to break
from its lines and let a strange language rise up.

Saturday

Each poem is waiting on its own Day of Pentecost
to thrash, to *robosei* and *yashundai*,
and the poem will not care that some walk past,
afraid of the words we try out on our tongues
hoping this finally is the language of God,
that he might hear it and respond.

Kei Miller

This poem, about witnessing women's Pentecostal worship in the Caribbean, is a striking and passionate evocation of the profound, wild longing that can underlie both the act of praying and that of trying to make poetry. This longing is both utterly compelling and virtually impossible to articulate.

The poem describes the experience of a small boy who is dragged reluctantly to 'meet the Lord' by his grandmother, and in the Pentecostal gathering witnesses behaviour that both appals him (his grandmother becomes someone who abandons all respectability) and fascinates him (she is like a power of nature, an earthquake, and she cries out in a language unknown to human reason). Later, as an adult, he recalls a conversation where someone disparages this kind of 'speaking in tongues' as deluded gibberish. But the poet would want to take the cynic to witness the women's powerful praying, 'pulling up fresh words' from the dust, and ask him – isn't the poet doing something similar, risking innovation in language, new 'words we try out on our tongues/ hoping this finally is the language of God'.

With regard to the worship, the poet locates himself as both within and without: present, observing but not quite participating. He has to be 'dragged' there, yet this is the start of a 'heritage of standing spellbound/ as women worship.' The word 'outskirts' wonderfully sums up both the place where the poet stands, and the sight of the women's skirts flaring and blossoming as their bodies become abandoned in prayer. There is a similar wordplay on the word 'unbecoming', which conveys the process by which his grandmother lets go of her orderly task-oriented self, but also suggests the boy's disapproval of the 'conduct unbecoming' he is seeing unfold.

The grandmother's descent into ecstatic prayer beyond normal language ('She became grunt and rumble') involves literally ending up on the ground with her shoes kicked off. But note that the poet, by this stage, has stopped describing what 'she' did and has started to generalize, thereby including himself and us in the point he is making: 'sounds/ you can only make when your shoes have fallen off/ and you're on the ground'.

The significance of the 'ground' reminds us of the biblical story of creation, where human beings were created out of the dust of the earth, and of the start of Lent, where we are encouraged to remember that we are made of earth and will return to it. The worshipping woman in this poem becomes 'all earthquake', and the poem keeps returning to the image of women who are back embracing the earth and crying out to God from the ground, and from the ground of their being. It is as if from this dust their new language is 'pulled'.

The poem includes some of the grunts and rumbles, the so-called gibberish: *raba, yashundai, robosei*. By themselves they have no meaning in the public language that we share, but in the context of this poem they stand for the longings we cannot articulate, the prayers we do not know how to say, which the Spirit helps us to utter (Romans 8.26).

The poem describes the poet's journey from appalled little boy to someone who now comprehends an embarrassing heritage of worship as encompassing what he himself is most deeply attempting to do with his life: 'what is language but a sound we christen?' The poems he writes are efforts at speaking to God and communicating to the world in a revelatory way: 'Each poem is waiting on its own Day of Pentecost'. (According to Acts 2, each hearer understood the inspired speech of the apostles as if hearing it in their own mother tongue.) The 'rational' friend who accuses the worshippers as deluded utterers of gibberish has missed the point about why people pray, and why they write poetry.

How does your prayer life compare to this image of 'pulling up fresh words' from the ground? Recall an example of worship you found embarrassing, and reflect on what it could teach you.

WEEK 2

'How can it need so agonized an effort?'

Struggle

Monday

———◆•●•◆———

Alas my Lord,
How should I wrestle all the livelong night
With Thee my God, my Strength and my Delight?

How can it need
So agonized an effort and a strain
To make Thy Face of Mercy shine again?

How can it need
Such wringing out of breathless prayer to move
Thee to Thy wonted Love, when Thou art Love?

Yet Abraham
So hung about Thine Arm outstretched and bared,
That for ten righteous Sodom had been spared.

Yet Jacob did
So hold Thee by the clenched hand of prayer
That he prevailed, and Thou didst bless him there.

Elias prayed,
And sealed the founts of Heaven; he prayed again
And lo, Thy Blessing fell in showers of rain.

Gulped by the fish,
As by the pit, lost Jonah made his moan;
And Thou forgavest, waiting to atone.

All Nineveh
Fasting and girt in sackcloth raised a cry,
Which moved Thee ere the day of grace went by.

The Church prayed on
And on for blessed Peter in his strait,
Till opened of its own accord the gate.

Yea, Thou my God
Hast prayed all night, and in the garden prayed
Even while, like melting wax, Thy strength was made.

Alas for him
Who faints, despite Thy Pattern, King of Saints:
Alas, alas, for me, the one that faints.

Lord, give us strength
To hold Thee fast, until we hear Thy Voice
Which Thine own know, who hearing It rejoice.

Lord, give us strength
To hold Thee fast until we see Thy Face,
Full Fountain of all Rapture and all Grace.

But when our strength
Shall be made weakness, and our bodies clay,
Hold Thou us fast, and give us sleep till day.

Christina Rossetti

It is traditional in Lent to devote special attention to our practice
of private prayer, which may have become routine, casual or quite
possibly virtually non-existent. The arresting image in the previous
prayer, about Pentecostal worshippers literally 'pulling words out
of dust' to offer to God, finds a kind of mirror in this poem about
private prayer.

Rossetti's poem explores the experience of prayer as an intense
struggle with God, which to the narrator is both painfully real and
somehow all wrong – an experience she shouldn't be having if what
she has been taught about God's nature is true. The first three stanzas
begin with the furious expostulation 'Alas my Lord', and repeated
questions as to why she should have this struggle and why it should
be necessary. The stanzas contrast a very physical human effort –
'wrestle all the livelong night'; 'So agonized an effort and a strain';

'Such wringing out of breathless prayer' – with the official qualities of God – 'my Strength and my Delight', 'Thy Face of Mercy', 'when Thou art Love'. Why this paradox of wrestling with a loving God?

But the next six stanzas turn on the word 'Yet'. Drawing on stories from the Bible, the poet, in vivid but economic couplets, recalls key characters who similarly had to engage in struggle to seek to achieve a blessing. Abraham's dialogue with God about the fate of Sodom (Genesis 18.22–33), is seen as a daring child who hangs on the arm of an enraged father to hold him back. Jacob's experience of wrestling all night with an angel (Genesis 32.22–32) is summed up as a 'clenched hand of prayer', a term that links him to the narrator. The poem moves through stories of Elijah (1 Kings 18.41–46), the disobedient prophet Jonah (Jonah 1—2), the people of Nineveh to whom he prophesied, and then to the story of Peter's imprisonment in the New Testament (Acts 12.3–17).

The climax of this series is introduced not by 'Yet' but by the affirmative 'Yea', as the narrator reaches a point of acceptance of the pattern. Jesus himself in the garden of Gethsemane (Luke 22.43–44) sweated with fear and prayed to avoid the suffering to come – a prayer which, in the wisdom of God and the plan of salvation, was not granted. So the second 'Alas' in the poem is directed not at God but at anyone who gives up on prayer, given that we have this model in front of us. Prayer that is painful and difficult, prayer that is indeed denied, may yet be crucial in the economy of salvation. It is the poem's narrator herself who is finally accused: 'Alas, alas, for me, the one that faints.'

The final stanzas offer us a surrendered attitude of prayer, made robust and credible because of the earlier argument with God, and the sense of standing in a powerful tradition. There is a prayer for strength 'To hold Thee fast, until we hear Thy Voice . . . see Thy Face', and that 'holding' has a real sense of physical struggle about it. Finally, the poem envisages the death of the one praying (beautifully implied by the image of strength being made weakness, see 2 Corinthians 12.9). God is asked to hold us fast 'and give us sleep till day' – and this holding implies tenderness and intimacy, as of a mother holding a sick or frightened child. The earthbound struggle of the poem is resolved into an image of eternal comfort, which because of what has come before is devoid of easy sentimentality about what the spiritual life entails.

Do you find prayer hard, and if so, how far does this poem help?

Tuesday

Affliction

Broken in pieces all asunder,
   Lord, hunt me not,
   A thing forgot,
Once a poor creature, now a wonder,
  A wonder tortured in the space
  Betwixt this world and that of grace.

My thoughts are all a case of knives,
   Wounding my heart
   With scatter'd smart;
As watering-pots give flowers their lives.
  Nothing their fury can control,
  While they do wound and prick my soul.

All my attendants are at strife,
   Quitting their place
   Unto my face:
Nothing performs the task of life:
  The elements are let loose to fight,
  And while I live, try out their right.

Oh, help, my God! let not their plot
   Kill them and me,
   And also thee,
Who art my life: dissolve the knot,
  As the sun scatters by his light
  All the rebellions of the night.

Then shall those powers, which work for grief,
> Enter thy pay,
> And day by day
Labour thy praise and my relief;
>> With care and courage building me,
>> Till I reach heaven, and much more, thee.

George Herbert

George Herbert writes with astonishing honesty and accuracy of detail about the struggle with what today we would probably call depression, and its impact on the spiritual life. This poem offers in telling images an analysis of how negative thoughts infect the heart and soul with hopelessness, and the poet prays to be released from these.

The theme is broached arrestingly in the first line; the poet is 'Broken in pieces all asunder' (rather like 'fragmented Adam' in Denise Levertov's poem, p. 10), and conceives of himself as not really human, not a proper creature, but something suspended between this world and the realm of grace. Referring to himself as a 'wonder' would, in seventeenth-century language, have implied something not 'wonderful' in the modern sense but rather monstrous, a thing to wonder at, a 'thing forgot'. Significantly, he begs God not to hunt him down – it is as if his very humanity is unrecognizable to the one who is the source of his being.

The second stanza throws up the acute image of his thoughts as 'all a case of knives' which continually cut and wound his heart. This is swiftly followed by a second image of a watering-pot that encourages plants to grow and rampage. Modern therapeutic practice often addresses the role of cumulative, self-feeding, destructive thoughts in trapping people in a cycle of gloomy, despairing feelings from which they feel unable to escape and act.

The third verse imagines the poet's faculties (presumably reason, good humour, motivation to address tasks or look after himself) as servants who are fighting each other and resigning from their roles, so that the 'task of life' is never properly addressed. Many who have suffered mental distress of various kinds will recognize this sense of continual inner conflict, and the exhausting sense that just getting on with the task of living from day to day is impossible.

But the next verse begins the 'turn' and the resolution in its plea to God to 'dissolve the knot'. The poet pleads from within the conflict not to be killed by it, nor yet to have his sense of God's presence destroyed. The image here is of God's presence as like the return of the sun that scatters shadow and 'All the rebellions of the night'. There is a strong biblical resonance here, for God is called the 'dawn from on high' (Luke 1.78), but there is also a beautiful accuracy about how it is at night that despair reaches its depths, accompanied by insomnia and anxieties that may disperse with the morning. The word 'rebellions' works hard, as it implies all this but also suggests the internal conflicts the poet has been describing – and quite possibly the poet's sense of rebellion against God who seems so absent and unrecognizable within despair.

Finally, the poet pleads that the negative thoughts that have captured all his faculties may be employed instead by God – 'Enter thy pay', and put their energy not into the grip of grief but into building up the suffering poet. How far this is a confident expectation, and how far a desperate hope, is hard to say. But instead of knives and wounds, the stanza foresees daily care and courage that both offer praise to God and bring relief to the one struggling in prayer. It is as if the poet gets hold of his thoughts and demands to know who they are really working for. When their intention is rightly aligned, integrity and spiritual well-being should be restored.

In what ways do your thoughts sometimes undermine your sense of God's presence? What are your strategies for dealing with them?

Wednesday

It is dangerous to read newspapers

While I was building neat
castles in the sandbox,
the hasty pits were
filling with bulldozed corpses

and as I walked to the school
washed and combed, my feet
stepping on the cracks in the cement
detonated red bombs.

Now I am grownup
and literate, and I sit in my chair
as quietly as a fuse

and the jungles are flaming, the under-
brush is charged with soldiers,
the names on the difficult
maps go up in smoke.

I am the cause, I am a stockpile of chemical
toys, my body
is a deadly gadget,
I reach out in love, my hands are guns,
my good intentions are completely lethal.

Even my
passive eyes transmute
everything I look at to the pocked
black and white of a war photo,
how
can I stop myself

Wednesday

It is dangerous to read newspapers.

Each time I hit a key
on my electric typewriter,
speaking of peaceful trees

another village explodes.

Margaret Atwood

It is traditional in Lent to contemplate one's own sinfulness and to seek to repent and turn around one's life. The two previous poems consciously address internal struggles with prayer or despair, reaching in each case a resolution that rests on surrender to God and trust in God's safe-keeping. This more contemporary poem takes a very different approach to exploring the sense of being a culpable person located in a violent world.

The poem works in several ways at once. Even the title, 'It is dangerous to read newspapers', is shot through with irony and absurdity, but there is an underlying seriousness and even terror that comes through. The narrator of the poem imagines herself to be so connected to the world which is fraught with dangers that she has some responsibility for what happens. As a child playing or walking to school, as an adult reading the newspaper or engaging in writing a book, or reaching out to others with good intentions, it is as if she unintentionally causes detonations and explosions through her attention to and fear of what is going on in the outside world of war.

The poem starts with the conscientious small girl 'building neat/ castles in the sandbox' which somehow feel connected with 'bulldozed corpses' (perhaps prompted by the shocking newsreels of the Jewish holocaust of the Second World War). She walks to school practising the traditional child's game of trying to avoid stepping on the cracks, but her fears about failure are enormous. There is a grotesque contrast between the respectably 'washed and combed' child, and the 'red bombs' that seem to be detonated when she steps on the cracks.

Later, as a grown-up sitting still, her apparent serenity is only the quietness of 'a fuse' in the moments before an explosion happens. Now there is a different war raging in the jungles, the landscape and greenery 'charged with soldiers'. Deadly smoke and chemical weapons are involved, perhaps in the jungles of Vietnam. This time the narrator affirms her good intentions towards the suffering, but instead of being able to do good she experiences a surreal sense that her body itself is a deadly weapon, her hands are guns, her intentions lethal. Even her 'passive eyes' seem to turn everything she looks at into an image of war. The 'pocked/ black and white' photo recalling disturbing visual accounts of wartime horrors over decades which neither she nor the reader can forget – we supply our own memories of the most vivid and famous newspaper images: Auschwitz, Hiroshima, My Lai and others. And even the brisk tapping of her typewriter key (writing of peace) feels like the trigger for yet another village somewhere across the world to be destroyed.

At one level, the poem is describing paranoia, since the narrator is not causally responsible for any of the events that haunt her steps. But at another, this sense of helpless, repeated and inevitable involvement in violent and brutal events that recur daily and yet unpredictably is familiar to anyone who reads newspapers and watches television news with their hearts and sympathies engaged. This is why 'It is dangerous to read newspapers', because one's human compassion and fellow feeling with suffering are constantly primed, yet no productive response seems possible and the next day will simply bring us news of another atrocity. For no previous generation has it been so possible to be vividly and immediately aware of the details of human cruelty and suffering taking place in the same world as we are currently inhabiting.

We are left without a resolution, uncomfortably reflecting on what our own responsibilities are, in this continuingly sinful and violent world. Given that our hands are not literally guns, or our intentions lethal, what is our involvement? On whose behalf are the unending wars of our generation being fought, and do we let them touch us? How can we genuinely repent and seek forgiveness, rather than simply try to avoid those pages in the newspapers? What does it mean to open ourselves to pray in a world where we are aware of these things?

Read the newspaper slowly and attentively, not missing out the painful stories. Pray for the people and contexts you read about.

Thursday

A Poison Tree

I was angry with my friend:
I told my wrath, my wrath did end.
I was angry with my foe:
I told it not, my wrath did grow.

And I water'd it in fears,
Night and morning with my tears:
And I sunned it with smiles,
And with soft deceitful wiles.

And it grew both day and night,
Till it bore an apple bright.
And my foe beheld it shine,
And he knew that it was mine.

And into my garden stole,
When the night had veil'd the pole;
In the morning glad I see
My foe outstretch'd beneath the tree.

William Blake

Like Atwood's poem, 'A Poison Tree' explores and lays bare personal human culpability. However, in the previous poem the events referred to were real, even if the connections between the events and the narrator were surreal and created by an all-pervasive sense of guilt. Here, the events narrated are not literally true, but are a kind of fable. However, there is here a tightly plotted causal sequence that has the ring of psychological truth about it.

Blake's 'Songs of Innocence and Experience' have a mislead-ingly childish form and tone to them. Accessible to children (and accurate about the darker side of real children's feeling life), they nevertheless have the power to startle adult readers and leave us pondering lines and rhymes that on the face of it are simple and even bland.

The poem is explicitly in the form of a confession, describing behaviour and the handling of relationships and what the outcomes have been. The subject is anger. Counter-intuitively, the narrator contrasts friendship and enmity not by the respective absence or presence of anger but by the freedom to name anger or to let it fester without being named. The anger with the friend disappears; it has gone by the end of the second line. The anger with the foe remains, and grows, taking over the whole of the rest of the poem with its energy and insidious life.

Notice the distinct responsibility the narrator takes for what happens, in the numerous statements that begin with 'I': 'I told my wrath', 'I told it not', 'I water'd it', 'I sunned it'. The anger has become like a plant taking hold, and the narrator's feelings and behaviour – tears and wiles – are like the rain and the sun (normally seen as God's province to provide). The behaviour does not seem to be aggressive, but rather 'soft' – self-protective and conciliatory. It is born of fear and involves false accommodation (smiles). The key is that it hides reality and deceives the foe into imagining that the narrator is not dangerous or hostile.

By the third stanza, the anger has its own powerful growth and does not need the nurturing any more. Interestingly, when fruit is produced it is beautiful, bright and shining, rather than something that betrays the bitterness of its origin. In the apple, Blake is evoking layers of other, older stories about fruit that simultaneously attracts and betrays: the forbidden fruit of the tree of the knowledge of good and evil in the garden of Eden, which led to the Fall; possibly also the golden apple of the Hesperides, which Paris had to award to one of three goddesses in the classical tale – an act that began the sequence of events leading to the Trojan Wars. The final line of this stanza is telling: 'he knew that it was mine.' Ironically, the fruit that is born of the narrator's bitterness is mistaken by the foe for a prize; his own envy is used to manipulate his downfall.

The outcome of the final paragraph is of a piece with the passive aggression of the earlier part of the poem. Without lifting a hand in anger, the narrator has persuaded the enemy to poison himself through seeking to steal the fruit. It is all done in darkness, after long nurturing of anger but without overt action. And the final accuracy about the nature of hatred is the pleasure taken in revenge: 'glad I see/ My foe outstretch'd beneath the tree.'

In this confessional poem there appears to be no repentance or even a sense of guilt. But this is not a monologue where the reader understands more than the narrator does about his motivations. It has a spare accuracy about each part of the sequence that would not be possible to someone who is still self-deceived. Many readers find that the poem echoes in the mind. It resonates with our experience of relationships that have the potential to go wrong, warning us to notice where truthfulness is lacking and enabling us to have the courage to interrupt the vicious sequence that unspoken anger can cause.

Recall a relationship where you have stoked anger or let it fester. Is there anything you could do now to resolve things?

Friday

---

*'Justus quidem tu es, Domine, si disputem tecum; verumtamen justa
loquar ad te: Quare via impiorum prosperatur?' Etc.*

Thou art indeed just, Lord, if I contend
With thee; but, sir, so what I plead is just.
Why do sinners' ways prosper? and why must
Disappointment all I endeavour end?
    Wert thou my enemy, O thou my friend,
How wouldst thou worse, I wonder, than thou dost
Defeat, thwart me? Oh, the sots and thralls of lust
Do in spare hours more thrive than I that spend,
Sir, life upon thy cause. See, banks and brakes
Now, leavèd how thick! lacèd they are again
With fretty chervil, look, and fresh wind shakes
Them; birds build – but not I build; no, but strain,
Time's eunuch, and not breed one work that wakes.
Mine, O thou lord of life, send my roots rain.

Gerard Manley Hopkins

Hopkins, a Roman Catholic priest and religious, used poetry to
wrestle with matters of faith and in particular with his own spiritual
journey, including the frustrations and hardships of his vocation. In
this he was very much a successor to George Herbert, who also frequently addressed God directly in his poetry, in a spirit of argument
as much as in obedience.

This poem is formally a Petrarchan sonnet, with its contrast between the first eight lines (the octave) and the last six (the sestet). It also includes the very carefully patterned rhyme scheme that is traditional in this form (ABBA, ABBA, CDCDCD), and it is a testament to the poet's skill that he manages to achieve this pattern without sacrificing the almost conversational style of the monologue.

In the octave, the belligerent approach to God has a strong biblical resonance. The Latin quotation at the head of the poem is from Jeremiah 12.1–2 ('You will be in the right, O LORD, when I lay charges against you; but let me put my case to you. Why does the way of the guilty prosper?' Etc.), and the poem begins as a meditation on that passage. As in the book of Job, Jeremiah contains a series of poems in which the prophet protests vigorously to God about the suffering that his prophetic call has brought him, and the comparative prosperity of the wicked and the treacherous. Like Jeremiah (or Job), the poet wants the matter debated as if in a court of law – God is required to demonstrate justice, but also to recognize the justice of his complaint. The cry, 'Why do sinners' ways prosper?' is a continuing theme within many of the psalms as well. So the narrator of the poem is locating himself in exalted biblical company, to protest the 'disappointment' that accompanies 'all I endeavour'. He just doesn't seem to be achieving very much and he is heartbroken.

The rant against God continues, who apparently could not be treating him worse if he were an enemy rather than a friend. Again, this is a traditional idea within the religious life, but not everyone has expressed it with such a sense of self-absorbed desolation. St Teresa of Avila, who experienced many hardships and setbacks, is said once to have wryly remarked to God, 'If this is how you treat your friends, no wonder you have so few!'

Such self-aware humour is absent from the narrator of the octave, and indeed, he goes on to castigate some particular sinners – 'the sots and thralls of lust' – who nevertheless seem to thrive more than he does, although he has dedicated his life to God's cause. It is interesting that he picks out 'lust' as the key sin; perhaps it is the vocation to celibacy that is proving so hard. There may be an echo of the self-righteous prayer of the Pharisee about the sinner (Luke 18.9–14).

The furious 'Sir' starts the first half line of the sestet, as if the complaint of the octave has spilled over into what should now be the different tone and direction of the sestet. And in the middle of that line, a totally different beginning is made. Here, there are echoes of Job. Job demands an answer from God, but he receives no answer about the justice or otherwise of his suffering. When God replies, it is to direct his attention to the wonders of creation. And in this poem, it is as if the poet suddenly asks the petulant voice in him to cease looking inwards on his disappointments and focus instead on the burgeoning of life in the return of spring that is happening around him.

In a few choice words, Hopkins calls up a sense of the surging natural life – leaves are 'thick', banks laced with 'fretty chervil', the fresh winds shaking the foliage. And it is at this point that the speaker in the poem is able to state poignantly what his heartbreak is really about: 'birds build – but not I build; no, but strain,/ Time's eunuch, and not breed one work that wakes.' His celibacy means that he will never literally breed offspring, and it seems that other endeavours that might also be seen as giving birth to fruitful work for God have never taken off.

And so the final line is able, in a quite different tone from the closed and self-righteous beginning, to utter a real prayer of petition that is open, vulnerable, and to the point: 'Mine, O thou lord of life, send my roots rain.'

Do you feel any envy for the achievements of others compared with your own? Being honest about this, use the last line of the poem as a prayer.

Saturday

The Wrong Beds

Life is a hospital ward, and the beds we are put in
are the ones we don't want to be in.
We'd get better sooner if put over by the window.
Or by the radiator, one could suffer easier there.

At night, the impatient soul dreams of faraway places.
The Aegean: all marble and light. Where, upon a beach
as flat as a map, you could bask in the sun like a lizard.

The Pole: where, bathing in darkness, you could watch
the sparks from Hell reflected in a sky of ice. The soul
could be happier anywhere than where it happens to be.

Anywhere but here. We take our medicine daily,
nod politely, and grumble occasionally.
But it is out of our hands. Always the wrong place.
We didn't make our beds, but we lie in them.

Roger McGough

Complaint about one's lot is also the theme of this poem, although
the tone seems more resigned and less intense than in the preceding
poem by Hopkins. There is a framework of irony – the slightly saucy
title turns out to herald not a French farce but some quite routine
grumbling you might find going on in any ordinary hospital ward.

The poem begins with a straightforward metaphor for life – it's
like a hospital ward. The proposition is rather like Shakespeare's
character who bluntly asserts that 'all the world's a stage'. The choice
of location means that, interestingly, there is no perceived need for

agonizing about why suffering should happen. Since we are all in hospital, suffering is obviously a 'given' – we wouldn't be there at all if it were not a pre-condition of our existence as hospital patients. The argument is all about where exactly. We can hear the plaintive tones of the patients who want the choice spots over by the window or the radiator; 'one could suffer easier there'. It is well known that in an NHS hospital you get the bed you are allocated and how exactly you might achieve one that suits you better is a mystery beyond your power as a patient to solve.

So the heart of this poem is not whether or why we suffer, but how we handle our suffering. In the next two stanzas, the poem's narrator (no doubt a patient) seems to use his imagination to let his correspondingly 'impatient' soul escape altogether from the dreary confines of the ward to exotic 'faraway places', whether full of light and heat or dramatically cold and dark. In either place, he imagines himself lying flat, as he is in his bed, but in a positive and exciting way. Either he is basking in the sun like a lizard, or he is 'bathing in darkness', gazing up at a dark, star-filled Arctic sky. The images of light and darkness may also hint at different moral choices: basking in good feelings or exulting in bad ones. But both are fantasies. This escapism is a familiar strategy for dealing with physical pain and fear – always more marked at night-time in hospital when sleep is hard to come by. The imagery and tone of these stanzas has a romantic quality quite different from the conversational grumbling of the beginning and end of the poem.

The key assertion of the poem seems to be that 'The soul/ could be happier anywhere than where it happens to be.' Of course, when you think about this proposition, it is completely impossible to test. It is a very recognizable feeling, and on the face of it sounds reasonable, but in fact it is the ultimate excuse for why we don't do our lives very well, and don't do our suffering very bravely. I think the poet is underlining this by the ironic pairing of sounds in 'could be happier' and 'happens to be'.

So, instead of getting on with inhabiting properly the actual present moment and location we are in, we shrug 'Anywhere but here', grumble mildly, endure mindlessly ('take our medicine') and take up residence in a permanent excuse. Engagement, patience, compassion or holiness – all possible responses to suffering – are beyond what can be expected of us, because we are in 'Always the wrong place'. Otherwise we could have been capable of rising to it, but it is not our fault, 'it is out of our hands.' Or so we say.

With brilliant economy, the final line sums the matter up while turning the narrator's position on its head. 'We didn't make our beds' – reversing the old proverb – sounds as if the poet is letting us off the hook. However, the double meaning of the phrase 'we lie in them' pins our self-deception wriggling on the page.

Reflect on where life has placed you, and whether you are fully inhabiting this, or wishing you were elsewhere. Try counting your blessings, but also clarifying what you have the power to change, if change is needed.

WEEK 3

'At home in the house of the living'

Being where we are

Monday

————•◆•————

Pax

All that matters is to be at one with the living God
to be a creature in the house of the God of Life.

Like a cat asleep on a chair
at peace, in peace
and at one with the master of the house, with the mistress,
at home, at home in the house of the living,
sleeping on the hearth, and yawning before the fire.

Sleeping on the hearth of the living world
yawning at home before the fire of life
feeling the presence of the living God
like a great reassurance
a deep calm in the heart
a presence
as of the master sitting at the board
in his own and greater being,
in the house of life.

D. H. Lawrence

The poems for this week are chosen to focus on being who we are –
having a realistic estimate of ourselves in the presence of God and of
each other, and inhabiting our place in the world fully and comfort-
ably.

This appealing image of a relaxed cat as an image of the self could
hardly be in greater contrast with what has been presented in some
of the previous poems: Adam distracted by the 'whirling rides'; the
narrator in Herbert's poem 'Affliction' whose thoughts are 'a case of

knives'; the one who finds it is 'dangerous to read newspapers', or the complaining patients who imagine that they would achieve peace of mind if they were 'Anywhere but here'.

Interestingly, it similarly contrasts with the other poem where sitting by the fire features ('The Call', p. 24). In the earlier poem, sitting in a torpid fashion before a sinking fire is an image of dullness and decline. But in Lawrence's poem, the profound relaxation of the cat before the hearth is about contemplation and being fully in the presence of God and of the present moment. To anyone who has watched a cat extend its whole body in ecstatic sleep, exposing the fur of its impossibly long belly to the warmth of an open fire, the image is compelling. It is the antithesis of any sort of hunched-up, fearful prayer; rather the animal arches itself to experience the greatest possible pleasure from the presence of the fire. It may not understand what causes the warmth it enjoys, but it intends to receive maximum advantage from this source of life.

The poem is like a hymn to contented creatureliness. To be at one with God is to be profoundly 'at home'; this very ordinary image of domesticity, through soothing repetitions ('at peace, in peace', 'at home, at home') creates in the reader a sense of peacefulness. A cat is a good indicator of whether a home is peaceful, whether there is tension, fear or anger around, since the animal can move from sleep to alertness very quickly. This cat, through its untroubled, yawning sleep, declares that all in the home is well. Thus it is that sleep itself is an assertion of life – the house of life is one that can be slept in, unafraid.

There are several repetitions of the theme of life: it is 'the house of the God of Life', 'the house of the living', 'the hearth of the living world', 'the fire of life'. Together, the cat and the fire symbolize a chain of being, a realm of material and animal creatures that belong together. The human reader is invited to perceive themselves as invited into the world as a homely home, sustained by the presence of God, an environment that they can feel comfortable to inhabit, enjoy, and even luxuriate in, feeling reassured like a sleeping cat.

Whether this sort of contemplation can ever be as simple for a human being, beset by complex thoughts and worries, as it is for a feline, hard-wired to relax fully when not out hunting, is open to debate. But as an image of contemplative prayer it is rich and original.

When, if ever, did you last feel like this cat when you were praying?

Tuesday

Friends' Meeting House, Frenchay, Bristol

When the doors of the house are shut,
Eyes lidded, mouth closed, nose and ears
Doing their best to idle, fingers allowed out
Only on parole; when the lovely holy distractions,
Safe scaffolding of much-loved formulae,
Have been rubbed away; then the plant
Begins to grow. It is hard to rear,
Rare herb of silence, through which the Word comes.
Three centuries of reticent, meticulous lives
Have naturalised it on this ground.

And the herb is the Vine, savage marauder,
That spreads and climbs unstoppably,
Filling the house, the people, with massing insistent shoots
That leaf through windows and doors, that rocket through
    chimneys,
Till flesh melts into walking forms of green,
Trained to the wildness of Vine, which exacts
Such difficult witness; whose work is done
In hopeless places, prisons, workhouses,
In countinghouses of respectable merchants,
In barracks, collieries, sweatshops, in hovels
Of driven and desperate men.
                              It begins here
In the ground of silence.

U. A. Fanthorpe

This poem forms an interesting comparison to the previous poem, 'Pax'. Instead of a sensuous, animal image for contemplative prayer, this detailed description of the communal silence of a Quaker meeting suggests that the senses have to be shut down before the power of prayer can take effect. Yet both are compelling images of fully inhabiting the present place and the present moment – the cat before the fire through its instinctive capacity to relax, the human beings in the meeting through the disciplined cultivation of openness to the Spirit through the avoidance of easy distraction. It is the steady refusal to fall into the grumbling fallacy of the patients in 'the wrong beds' – here is where they are, and where the word of power will be felt, if at all. In the first line there may be a reference to the gathering of the disciples behind closed doors, waiting in prayer before the Spirit descends on them at Pentecost (Acts 2.2).

The poem is written as if the meeting house itself is sentient, and is itself the subject of the effort to pray. Of course, in reality it is the members of the meeting who shut their eyes and mouths, seek to calm the senses of smell or hearing, move their fingers minimally, and only if they really must. This calm stanza stresses the need to delete agitation, arousal or distraction, paying tribute to the 'Three centuries of reticent, meticulous lives' of earlier Friends who have similarly held silence in this place. Not only the immediate sensory inputs but the 'lovely holy distractions' of 'much-loved formulae' – those passionate and beautiful words generated by human beings to express spiritual truths – must be let go. The poet imagines them as a kind of scaffolding: once necessary to construct the building but now strictly irrelevant, and taking up wall space that needs to be available for something else to grow, a 'Rare herb' that through careful cultivation of the ground has been 'naturalised' here – rather like snowdrops or cyclamen that a gardener hopes will start to grow year by year rather than need new bulbs to be planted again and again.

The second stanza initially takes the reader by surprise after this calming, almost repressed first stanza with its promise of a tender herb, 'hard to rear' in the silence. For the herb turns out to be a rampant Vine, 'savage marauder', wild and invasive, growing unbelievably fast and penetrating all over the fabric of the house. The poet is here taking the blandly familiar biblical image of the vine (John 15.1–6) and subverting it to shock and surprise, with its astonishing energy. However, anyone who has a garden plant that is related to a vine can bear witness that its growth each year can be phenomenal if not carefully controlled. Starting from spurs that look frankly wizened and dead in spring, a vine throws out long stems of climbing greenery, sustained by roots that go hugely deep. It can quickly colonize whole trees or buildings.

The poet imagines the power and wildness of the Vine's energy sending forth the humans in the building to go and perform a 'difficult witness' in the other places of the world where things happen or people suffer – amid industry, trade and banking; in places of desperation and poverty. Attention to being present in this significant place will release the power and resilience to change things in quite other places. This is the other side of the Quaker witness: the withdrawing to silence is counterbalanced by the testimony of committed action for justice in hard contexts.

What opportunities do you make to spend time in silence and pay attention to the Spirit, and how might you extend these?

Wednesday

———◆◆◆———

i am a little church(no great cathedral)
far from the splendor and squalor of hurrying cities
– i do not worry if briefer days grow briefest,
i am not sorry when sun and rain make april

my life is the life of the reaper and the sower;
my prayers are prayers of earth's own clumsily striving
(finding and losing and laughing and crying)children
whose any sadness or joy is my grief or my gladness

around me surges a miracle of unceasing
birth and glory and death and resurrection:
over my sleeping self float flaming symbols
of hope,and i wake to a perfect patience of mountains

i am a little church(far from the frantic
world with its rapture and anguish)at peace with nature
– i do not worry if longer nights grow longest;
i am not sorry when silence becomes singing

winter by spring,i lift my diminutive spire to
merciful Him Whose only now is forever:
standing erect in the deathless truth of His presence
(welcoming humbly His light and proudly His darkness)

E. E. Cummings

This is another poem where a building is treated as if it were a sentient being; the voice of the 'little church' is the voice of the poem. A building clearly stays in one place. It suffers the passing weather and witnesses the fury and glory of the changing seasons. It inhabits a single landscape and observes the world from that perspective, and therefore can become, as in this poem, an image of being fully and undistractedly in the present, being 'at home' in the place where we are. It is an extraordinary and irony-free hymn to contentment with being oneself.

The assertion of being a 'little church(no great cathedral)' is significant for a building. Architecture is often a place where pretentious flourishes can feature, and rural churches are not exempt from this, especially when they have been constructed or restored by a wealthy donor with local neighbours to impress. But those who enjoy visiting churches will have experienced both the kind of place that wishes it were a cathedral, and the simpler churches where the lines of the building lead to an atmosphere of silence and worship rather than draw attention to themselves. We can aspire to the confidence and contentment necessary for us to proclaim happily: 'i am a little church'.

The first verse locates the little church in the countryside, far from splendour, squalor or 'hurry'. The soft sound of 'hurry' is echoed in the next two lines: 'i do not worry'; 'i am not sorry'. It is first defined by negatives: not large, not splendid or squalid, experiencing neither haste, nor worry, nor regret for the conditions it lives with 'when sun and rain make april'. The mingled weather of April is often E. E. Cummings' way of referring to the mixed joy and sorrow of human experience which is so fertile for the growth of love and wisdom.

Throughout the poem it is the external landscape in which the church stands that provides the backdrop to its sense of peacefulness with its existence. In the second stanza it is as if that landscape generates its own children. The poet characteristically stuffs a bracket with verbs that describe human activities, so that you have the sense of unceasing activity, again full of contrasts and extremes. You imagine generations, formed by the local landscape, living and dying. The humans served by the church are also 'little', yet all precious.

The next two stanzas celebrate the miracle of the surging seasons and the sequence of light and dark, this endless cycle of change circling the stable centre of the fixed and calm church – 'my sleeping self' and the 'perfect patience of mountains'. The proclamation of identity is asserted again, with variation. The church knows about rapture and anguish but is here at peace – untroubled by lengthening nights or briefer days, contented with either silence or singing.

This inhabiting of the present moment, day and night, season by season, leads to a beautiful articulation of contemplative prayer to 'merciful Him Whose only now is forever'. The last verse witnesses to the deep and fitting pride of creatures who have just estimates of their own 'diminutive' selfhood and yet, 'standing erect', understand their inestimable value in the eyes of God.

What is your favourite place? Try writing a journal entry in the 'voice' of that place.

Thursday

———•◆•———

The Moment

The moment when, after many years
of hard work and a long voyage
you stand in the centre of your room,
house, half-acre, square mile, island, country,
knowing at last how you got there,
and say, *I own this,*

is the same moment the trees unloose
their soft arms from around you,
the birds take back their language,
the cliffs fissure and collapse,
the air moves back from you like a wave
and you can't breathe.

No, they whisper. *You own nothing.*
You were a visitor, time after time
climbing the hill, planting the flag, proclaiming.
We never belonged to you.
You never found us.
It was always the other way round.

Margaret Atwood

This poem explores not the sense of contentment of inhabiting your
own place in the world, being 'at home' where you are, but rather
the discovery that an achievement of identity based on ownership is
completely illusory.

The first stanza of the poem apparently celebrates an important moment of achievement, after a long journey and years of hard work – perhaps building a career or business, establishing a stable household, working to understand your own psyche and feeling at last that you have grasped something to rely on. Yet the list of possible places you might be standing in begins to be worrying. First it is your 'room', then 'house, half-acre, square mile, island, country' – each possibility moving step-wise into ever more overweening amounts of space that you apparently command. There is a sense that no space would be enough; that there must always be more, as wealth and power accumulate. The key is that the self envisaged by the poem does not only grasp how they 'got there', but goes on to assert '*I own this*'; that is, it is mine, it cannot be taken away from me.

Without even finishing a sentence, the second stanza proclaims that, by contrast, this is the precise moment when everything will be taken away. Presumably at an individual level this might in fact be through illness, or bereavement, or business failure, or other catastrophe beyond our control. What we 'own' never survives the conditions of our mortality. Or it might be about a mid-life sense of losing a sense of our grasp on things just when we have apparently achieved all we thought we were striving for. On a global level, however, it is really about the earth itself. Humans have acted as if the planet's resources were infinitely exploitable, and we had the right to claim ownership of these.

But this is not the case, and this false claim will be found to have destroyed the relationship that implicitly did exist. The landscape is given human features: trees have 'soft arms' but they no longer embrace us. The birds used to communicate in language we understood, but they will do so no more. The mountain cliffs, seemingly so solid, will crack and collapse. The air itself is sucked away. The natural world we thought we inhabited and owned turns out to be something we ourselves depend on, but which we have already lost. We 'can't breathe' in the atmosphere we have polluted. We did not know the landscape was a living thing; we only see this in retrospect.

In the final stanza, the landscape speaks back to arrogant humanity. It is only a whisper, but it is all in the past tense. We completely misread the situation. We thought we were owners: in fact we were visitors. We imagined that we had discovered the significant places on our planet. We planted national flags to claim sovereignty. Reality was 'the other way round'; the earth gave rise to our life, and we depended on it. And we are only realizing this at the point where there may be no going back.

Or is the poem actually that bleak? I think that there is more than one way of reading the end of the poem, and I find a curious comfort in what the landscape says in its refusal to be owned. For it implies that the human being, while denied the apparent security of owner-ship of space, is in fact 'found' by the earth. To accept the reality of our dependence on the earth could be exhilarating rather than fearful. It could be one further step on the journey of discovery and acceptance, as Mary Oliver puts it in her poem 'Wild Geese', about our 'place/ in the family of things'.

What do you feel you own? Consider your assets, job, family, property, achievements, memories, and so on. Does it matter if you don't really own them?

Friday

Rembrandt's Late Self-Portraits

You are confronted with yourself. Each year
The pouches fill, the skin is uglier.
You give it all unflinchingly. You stare
Into yourself, beyond. Your brush's care
Runs with self-knowledge. Here

Is a humility at one with craft.
There is no arrogance. Pride is apart
From this self-scrutiny. You make light drift
The way you want. Your face is bruised and hurt
But there is still love left.

Love of the art and others. To the last
Experiment went on. You stared beyond
Your age, the times. You also plucked the past
And tempered it. Self-portraits understand,
And old age can divest,

With truthful changes, us of fear of death.
Look, a new anguish. There, the bloated nose,
The sadness and the joy. To paint's to breathe,
And all the darknesses are dared. You chose
What each must reckon with.

Elizabeth Jennings

Jennings' poem needs to be read with the visual image of Rembrandt's series of later self-portraits in mind. Since he was a young man, the artist had regularly painted himself. In the earlier portraits, he is shown wearing different costumes, glancing over his shoulder in an assertive pose, as if he is trying on different personas as an ambitious young man. But the later portraits seem to gaze out at the viewer with a straightforward gaze, full of directness and honesty about life's bruises and the inevitable advance of old age.

The artist must have used a mirror in the process of depicting his own face, and the poet makes this honest visual self-assessment stand for the kind of truthful self-examination that is particularly appropriate in the season of Lent. She addresses Rembrandt as if she were speaking to him across the ages: 'You are confronted with yourself.' In the first stanza she focuses, as the artist must have done in preparing his initial sketches, on what the man looks like at this point in time. The marks of age, greater than last year, are examined dispassionately. His ruthless self-estimation is depicted by the detail of his brushwork, as the alliteration highlights: 'Your brush's care/ Runs with self-knowledge.' No airbrushing is permitted.

The second stanza examines the integration of humility with the skill of the artist's craft. He can both form a truthful estimate of himself and reproduce it visually. Arrogance and pride are set aside in the interests of truth. And yet there must have been a pride in his astonishing artistic capacity, which seems to echo that of the Creator: 'You make light drift/ The way you want.' In the same way, the eyes of the subject under examination show life's wounds but also its consolations and wisdom: 'Your face is bruised and hurt/ But there is still love left.'

The third stanza places Rembrandt in the great tradition of artists before and since, who have worked in an experimental way, without excluding themselves from the scrutiny of their art. It makes him accessible as a mentor for later times, as he stared intently not just at himself but at himself as a human being whose experience was capable of touching lives in quite other contexts: 'You stared beyond/ Your age, the times.' The direct address to the artist as 'you' conveys this sense of a relationship, with the narrator of the poem being positively helped in his or her own self-estimate by what the artist has achieved.

Scrupulous attention to the reality of flaws and to the passing of time, though astringent, is curiously comforting as well. When all has been exposed and truthfully declared, a kind of reclaiming of the past takes place: 'You also plucked the past/ And tempered it. Self-portraits understand'.

The final stanza asserts that this honesty not only tempers the past, but through the charting of ageing can remove our fear of the death that lies ahead of us. There is a new mood in this stanza – instead of bluntly accusing the face of ugliness, there is almost a casual shrug of recognition for both the pain in the face and its enlarged nose: 'Look, a new anguish. There, the bloated nose'. There is an acceptance of the reality of both with equanimity; this is the deal in human life, that we experience pain and we get relentlessly older. But these facts are not depressing; they and their depiction are the very stuff of life. Nothing is beyond contemplation for someone like Rembrandt, who is truthful enough to know himself well, and skilled enough to articulate the truth in his craft. This is what makes life worth living: 'To paint's to breathe,/ And all the darknesses are dared'.

Find some photos of yourself over a range of years, including some that you are not that keen on. What do they tell you about your character?

Saturday

The Trees

The trees are coming into leaf
Like something almost being said;
The recent buds relax and spread,
Their greenness is a kind of grief.

Is it that they are born again
And we grow old? No, they die too.
Their yearly trick of looking new
Is written down in rings of grain.

Yet still the unresting castles thresh
In fullgrown thickness every May.
Last year is dead, they seem to say,
Begin afresh, afresh, afresh.

Philip Larkin

Since Lent comes in spring in the northern hemisphere, often starting when the trees are in bud and ending at Easter with the sprout-
ing of new green leaves, it is hard to resist seeing parallels between
the cycles of nature and the spiritual journey at this time of year.
This deceptively simple poem is not explicitly exploring Christian
themes, but life and death, and the capacity to live life fully even with
the knowledge of death's reality is at its heart. It both invites us to
compare ourselves with the yearly cycle of the trees, and also denies
us a simple 'reading off' of a moral. Each word of this apparently
conversational poem works hard.

In the first stanza, the coming into leaf is 'Like something almost being said'. The phrase either suggests that intuitive communication which can happen between people who know each other well, or else it refers to the human desire to attribute to nature a capacity to teach us something. Is the greening of trees in spring (which we find so cheering and inspiring) making an announcement to us, or not? The next two lines produce another puzzle. The poet's choice of words about buds is accurate and visually vivid – 'The recent buds relax and spread', but then he asserts that their greenness 'is a kind of grief'. Why is the process of opening as the weather warms a kind of grief? Is it because there is a relentless process of ageing that moves from the tight and perfect bud, through to the death and fall of that leaf?

The next stanza picks up the theme of death, and specifically the sense that spring is about being 'born again', with the resonances for us about spiritual rebirth or resurrection. Here, the question contrasts the life of the tree and humanity's life, rather as the book of Job does: 'For there is hope for a tree, if it is cut down, that it will sprout again, and that its shoots will not cease . . . But mortals die, and are laid low; humans expire, and where are they?' (Job 14.7, 10). But that notion is immediately scotched: 'No, they die too.' Trees also age, as we do; even if they have a much longer life-span, they do eventually die. Our desire to see trees as perpetually renewed turns out to be a 'yearly trick of looking new', even as the actual years of the tree's life are recorded in the rings of grain of its trunk.

So the symbol whose apparent resurrection we are inspired by is revealed as deceptive and mortal too. And yet, as the last stanza affirms, we cannot help being moved by what the trees 'seem to say' rather than their botanical reality. This stanza is worth reading out loud, as the words, clustered thickly with sibilant consonants, sound like the noise of the trees wrestling with the gusting winds of spring. The image of the trees as 'castles' adds lots more 's' sounds, which creates this effect but also conveys the seeming solidity of the trees now that they are clothed again with their new leaves.

In spite of placing all sorts of cautions around our simple response to the greening of the trees, the poem ends with a threefold cry of hope – 'Begin afresh, afresh, afresh.' Even though we die, even though the trees too are ageing and will die, even though springtime is a trick of looking new, rather than a genuine resurrection, we can long to start afresh, with the sap rising in us. Mortality is the condition under which we live our lives; yet that does not prevent us from embracing genuine hope.

Have a walk and look closely at some trees.

WEEK 4

'A reckless way of going'
Facing suffering and death

Monday

Epitaph

Even such is Time, which takes in trust
Our youth, our joys, and all we have,
And pays us but with age and dust;
Who in the dark and silent grave,
When we have wandered all our ways,
Shuts up the story of our days:
And from which earth, and grave, and dust,
The Lord shall raise me up, I trust.

Sir Walter Ralegh

The poems selected for this week address head on the problem of mortality and human suffering. Contemplating one's death was in earlier centuries regarded as a religious duty, especially appropriate during Lent.

Prior to the mid twentieth century, mortality was a fairly constant presence in most people's lives; childbirth, for baby and mother, was a risky business, and many common infections had no effective treatment except bed rest before the discovery of antibiotics. Most homes would be familiar with nursing sick children or older people, and people died and were laid out at home rather than in hospitals.

Being well prepared for one's own death when the time came was considered important, because of the conviction that this was when the soul faced a critical moment of judgement about its eternal fate. Our contemporary generation does not much care to contemplate death at all, perhaps because many of us have no close experience of accompanying the dying. If anything, it is the fear of possible pain and indignity in the process of dying that preoccupies us, rather than fear for what might come after death. However, poets have tended to be prepared to address what is otherwise hard for us to think about.

Ralegh's 'Epitaph', said to have been written on the eve of his execution, captures exquisitely the beliefs of his age (sixteenth century) about time, mortality and the hope of eternal life. The poem begins almost as if we are in the middle of a conversation about Time and its passing, and the poet is replying to some thought already expressed by the reader. As an epitaph, the poem envisages the reader standing and gazing at the text written on a tombstone or burial plaque. So the mutual contemplation of an actual death is a 'given' and has been included in the meaning of the poem. It was common for an epitaph to address the one presumed to be reading it. It is a warning from the dead to the living, to take in the reality of death while there is still time to amend one's life.

Time, with a capital 'T', is thought of as a person with authority and agency, almost like a lawyer or a legal guardian, who has the power to take 'in trust' assets that are ours for the spending. Yet instead of working for our benefit and returning these assets with interest, Time 'pays us but with age and dust'. Youth is returned not as maturity but age; joys of various sorts turn to dust. The introduction of 'dust' leads on to the notion of the 'dark and silent grave' that awaits all of us – specifically the poet himself now, as his actual tomb lies before the reader. There is a sense that the person who lives through time has much less sense of direction and purpose than does 'Time' himself. While we are just wandering around, Time takes the initiative and 'Shuts up the story' – as if writing the definitive ending, the epitaph.

The poem is written as a single sentence, so we have the impression of a seamless progression of time, moving in a regular but unstoppable way, at least until we hit the end of line 6, 'Shuts up the story of our days:'. At this point there is a sense of pause, a downbeat moment which almost gives the impression that this is a contemporary writer, with a belief that we live and then we die and that's it. But then follows a triumphant couplet which reverses the implacable direction of time. The sense of confident faith is carried in every word. The powerful list, 'earth', 'grave', 'dust', which echoes but reverses the previous downward path, is followed by a straightforward declaration of faith in resurrection: 'The Lord shall raise me up, I trust.'

This is a trust about eternity. There is a lovely contrast with the deceptiveness of Time, who at the beginning of the poem took everything 'in trust' and then reneged on his promise. Remembering that the presumed narrator is now speaking to us from his tomb, this is a powerful declaration, and acts as a challenge to us who are still living to match such faith.

Have a go at writing your own epitaph.

Tuesday

The Soul's Garment

Great Nature clothes the soul, which is but thin,
With fleshly garments, which the Fates do spin;
And when these garments are grown old and bare,
With sickness torn, Death takes them off with care,
And folds them up in peace and quiet rest,
And lays them safe within an earthly chest:
Then scours them well and makes them sweet and clean,
Fit for the soul to wear those clothes again.

Margaret Cavendish

This poem, written a century after Ralegh's 'Epitaph', but still within a period when belief in bodily resurrection was a matter of course, has a much gentler tone, and there is not the same contrast between the destructive ravages of time and the promise of eternal life.

It is written by a woman, at a time when very few girls received an education and most women who did write would publish anonymously if at all. Interestingly, her account of the human conditions of ageing and mortality is attended by female figures and female activity – though we are talking of quite lowly activities, to do with the care of precious clothes.

First of all, it is not Time but 'Great Nature' who clothes the soul; and the 'fleshly garments' put on the naked soul are spun by the 'Fates'. Here, the classical Fates seem benevolent, like women who are weaving the layette for a new baby. (In classical myth, they are rather sinister, witch-like figures who operate blindly and are heartlessly inclined to take their shears to the thread of life that passes between them).

The body, understood as a garment, is then envisaged as growing old as garments do, becoming 'bare' and 'torn', and a third female figure, Death, 'takes them off with care'. Again, there is a sense of gentleness, as of a child's nurse or an adult woman's maid, undressing someone who is tired and unwell. The process of dying is seen as gentle and dignified, a time of peacefulness after the experience of being 'torn' with sickness.

The image of the garments is continued throughout the poem. The next phase – the laying out of the body and the funeral – is conveyed as if the clothes are being carefully folded and packed away. The 'earthly chest' is like a wooden linen chest where precious fabrics were folded and kept, but of course it refers to the wooden coffin which will be laid in earth.

Judgement and resurrection are imagined as the process of careful (if thorough) washing and mending, so that the garments may be worn again by the soul. Clothes were handmade and precious, and materials would have been handled carefully, made over and reused as much as possible. The soul, which is 'but thin', requires its own body to be clothed and recognized for eternity. The thought here is consistent with the biblical teaching about the resurrection of the body. St Paul imagines that 'we will all be changed' when the dead are raised, but that it will be (as Charles Wesley's hymn has it) 'from glory into glory' – each kind of creature having its own particular recognizable glory and resurrection (1 Corinthians 15.51, 41).

As an image of bodily resurrection, there is a domesticity here, but also a respect for the material body that is not always found in traditional Christian writings. The frail flesh in which the soul lives is not simply discarded, neither is it seen as falling into dust, but it is restored and returned, fit to wear for eternity, valued and precious.

In what ways do you love your body and take care of it? Do something today that is in the interests of your body's health and well-being.

Wednesday

Because I could not stop for Death –
He kindly stopped for me –
The Carriage held but just Ourselves –
And Immortality.

We slowly drove – He knew no haste
And I had put away
My labor and my leisure too,
For His Civility –

We passed the School, where Children strove
At Recess – in the Ring –
We passed the Fields of Gazing Grain –
We passed the Setting Sun –

Or rather – He passed Us –
The Dews drew quivering and chill –
For only Gossamer, my Gown –
My Tippet – only Tulle –

We paused before a House that seemed
A Swelling of the Ground –
The Roof was scarcely visible –
The Cornice – in the Ground –

Since then – 'tis Centuries – and yet
Feels shorter than the Day
I first surmised the Horses' Heads
Were toward Eternity –

Emily Dickinson

In this nineteenth-century poem we are apparently in the same territory as Ralegh's 'Epitaph', in the graveyard contemplating mortality, with assumptions about immortality and eternity. Yet the whole tone of the poem is utterly different.

Dickinson's poem is conversational, but is chatting about something that is really fraught with fear. Instead of a straightforward gazing at death, death is spoken about as if he were a gentleman offering a ride to a lady in his carriage – a momentary civility, which is part of the conventional dance of polite courtesies between the sexes in respectable provincial life. Because the woman who is the voice of the poem did not own her own carriage, he 'kindly stopped for me'. But the casual phrase 'I could not stop for Death' also refers to the narrator's sense of denial, her refusal to stop and contemplate this possibility. And the reader is clear that there is something sinister under the 'kindly' gesture – she did not have a choice about whether or not to get into the carriage.

This double-edged 'civility' is continued in the next stanza. The courteous driver, who 'knew no haste', is firmly in charge of the process. The narrator describes herself as responding in kind to the gentility of the occasion. However, what she has 'put away' is rather more significant than her embroidery, or whatever temporary pursuit was preoccupying her, in the interests of polite conversation during a ride together. She has let go of the whole of her life: 'My labor and my leisure too'.

The next stanza starts with a scene that could plausibly still be about passing through the village – the school at recess, the harvest fields – yet it ends in quite a different place: beyond the setting sun. The gentle ride has become like a review of the narrator's past (we note that the children in the playground are not playing but striving). The 'Gazing Grain' perhaps begins to suggest the biblical fields where angels are the reapers and it is human souls that are being harvested (Matthew 13.24–43).

Time has begun to function in strange ways in the next stanza. It is not clear whether the carriage passes the 'Setting Sun' or the other way around. It is becoming chilly and fearful. An entertaining afternoon ride out would not be continued beyond dewfall and nightfall.

And, in a surreal way, the woman realizes that she is dressed only in gossamer and tulle – fragile materials, which could imply either that she was dressed only for sunshine or that she is laid out for her funeral.

And then it is clear that the stopping place is indeed the graveyard. But the tomb is described as if it were some kind of rather puzzling house, with architectural features strangely positioned, very close to the ground. Thus the sense of denial implicit from the start, the refusal to call a spade a spade, is continued in polite (if bemused) comments about the roof and cornice of the building to which she has been conveyed.

The final stanza distances the whole event, as if all this has happened in the remote past, and the narrator is gently telling us about her adventure. And yet there is nothing gentle about the implication of the poem. Not only for her are the horses' heads firmly pointing towards Eternity. But there is an uncertainty about the concept of eternity that is absent in the previous two poems. We are left quietly in the graveyard, in a 'Swelling of the Ground', with just a surmise rather than a confident faith in the life to come.

What thought have you given to your own funeral? Think about some aspect of it (such as hymns, readings) and make a note for your executors.

Thursday

—————•◦•————

Deaths of Flowers

I would if I could choose
Age and die outwards as a tulip does;
Not as this iris drawing in, in-coiling
Its complex strange taut inflorescence, willing
Itself a bud again – though all achieved is
No more than a clenched sadness,

The tears of gum not flowing.
I would choose the tulip's reckless way of going;
Whose petals answer light, altering by fractions
From closed to wide, from one through many perfections,
Till wrecked, flamboyant, strayed beyond recall,
Like flakes of fire they piecemeal fall.

E. J. Scovell

This twentieth-century poem is a quite different take on death. Here there is no speculation at all about whether or not there is anything beyond death. Probably, since the poet has chosen to focus on something as evanescent as the life and death of flowers, the implication is that nothing beyond this life is envisaged.

But the poem focuses instead on how life, and especially the process of ageing, should be lived in the face of inevitable mortality after an all too short flourishing. The poet has observed closely how the blooms of different flowers – the tulip and the iris – respond to the process of ageing, either as garden plants or cut flowers. The narrator announces that she aspires to be like the tulip, ageing and dying 'outwards'.

With acute visual accuracy, she describes how the iris, after displaying its petals in a showy and generous way (irises are also called 'flags' because of their appearance), starts to draw itself in, ending up in a tight bunch once more. With a long sequence of hissing adjectives, the poet refers to its 'complex strange taut inflorescence' – a surreal kind of flowering inwards, or perhaps more properly a reversal of the flowering process towards a 'clenched sadness' that is unable to release the gummy stuff that accumulates around the one-time flower head. The break the poem makes in the middle of this sentence mirrors the lack of flow.

By contrast, the narrator declares: 'I would choose the tulip's reckless way of going'. Again, the detail of a tulip's process of ageing is meticulously charted. The petals open with the sunlight, and then partially close again at night-time, even when brought indoors as cut flowers – they 'answer light' in a responsive way. Thus over time their profile alters fractionally each day and, unlike the iris, all the stages have a beauty about them. At the final stage the petals do fall, but they do so with all their vibrant colour intact, 'like flakes of fire'. There is a flamboyant, spontaneous air about the ageing tulip – wrecked but magnificent – which inspires the observer even as it dies 'outwards'.

The contrasting flower images are maintained throughout the poem. It is left to the reader to do the application of these to the living of life as we age. Many older people are inclined to draw in their horns, being very careful, letting their interests and social contacts narrow, their political views solidify and perhaps even their compassion dry up. The poem sees this approach as achieving nothing but a self-hugging sadness towards the end, not weeping perhaps but also not relieved or comforted by the expression of sadness. It is not about ripeness and maturity but about a sort of hopeless effort at regression, just as the iris appears to be 'willing/ Itself a bud again'.

By contrast, the tulip's way may be 'reckless', but it seems to remain responsive, spontaneous, seeking the light and giving generously of itself. Nothing is drawn in and no colour is lost in the process of dying. There are those who seem to be able to move outwards rather than inwards towards the end, to retain an openness to new experiences and people, to risk everything but in fact not lose or diminish themselves as death approaches. The poem asks us to choose what kind of dying we want, and thus to choose how to live now.

How like the tulip are you? What needs to loosen up or open out?

Friday

On his blindness

When I consider how my light is spent
Ere half my days in this dark world and wide,
And that one talent which is death to hide
Lodged with me useless, though my soul more bent
To serve therewith my Maker, and present
My true account, lest He returning chide,
'Doth God exact day-labour, light denied?'
I fondly ask. But Patience, to prevent
That murmur, soon replies, 'God doth not need
Either man's work or his own gifts. Who best
Bear his mild yoke, they serve him best. His state
Is kingly: thousands at his bidding speed,
And post o'er land and ocean without rest;
They also serve who only stand and wait.'

John Milton

Contemplating the reality of death appropriately moves us to reflect on how we should live now, before we die. But for some of us (and as life expectancy increases, perhaps most of us will face this for a significant period as we age) there is a daily issue about how to live well with suffering, chronic pain or a life-limiting impairment. Milton famously had to endure blindness, probably caused by glaucoma, from mid-life until his death at the age of 66.

This poem uses the classic Petrarchan form (proposing a

dilemma in the first eight lines, and then an answer or a new direction in the final six), and keeps to the very disciplined rhyme structure at the end of the lines: ABBA, ABBA, CDECDE. In a way characteristic of Milton, he builds up, clause by clause, to the key question in line 7.

The first line lets us know that the narrator is blind, but by referring to 'my light' he implies not only that light is denied him but his own inner light is exhausted and spent. 'Ere half my days' – this is poignant, but also furious; there is no way that anyone can be sure that he is genuinely only halfway through his span of life. We have an impression of someone who feels strongly that he has potentially half his active life left, during which he was expecting to achieve some great work for God within an evil world: 'in this dark world and wide' – dark because it is full of wrongdoing, as well as literally always dark now to the narrator.

Clearly what rankles most is the sense of uselessness. What did the poet mean by 'that one talent which is death to hide'? Perhaps it is his scholarship and ability to influence events and people through his writing (though in fact for Milton himself this did not cease – *Paradise Lost* and several other works were dictated after he became blind). But leaving the 'talent' unnamed means that readers can identify with the poem's lament, whatever may be their own equivalent. Certainly the poet is referring to the biblical parable of the talents, in which the figure who is most criticized is the one who fearfully buries his talent (a large amount of silver) rather than invest it, or risk using it in some way (Matthew 25.24–30). The narrator imagines presenting his accounts as in the parable, and fearing to be judged for the same reason.

The ceaseless build-up of clauses conveys the sense of a troubled and complaining sufferer, not reconciled to his condition in any way. The question comes out as an explosion, reminiscent of Job's complaints about his sufferings: 'Doth God exact day-labour, light denied?' Interestingly, it is not the unfairness of the affliction itself that is attacked; it is whether or not the same delivery of work is expected under adverse circumstances. Is God a tyrant, demanding 'bricks without straw' such as the Egyptian Pharaoh required of the enslaved Israelites (Exodus 5.6–13)?

It is a good question. However, the poem immediately places the narrator as being in the wrong. He asks 'fondly' (that is, in a pettish and perverse way). And Patience takes up the whole of the sestet 'to prevent/ That murmur'. This phrase carefully smoothes over the transition from the octet to the sestet; the angry question is no sooner asked than it is comprehensively answered.

The first reply is that God does not actually need our work. This is a salutary reminder to the workaholic activist narrator who feels useless without the ability to develop his distinctive talent. The second is that serving God is done best by those who willingly take his 'yoke' on their shoulders, like an ox being willing to accept the wooden yoke in order to pull the plough, guided by the farmer. The reference is to Matthew 11.28–30, where Jesus invites his disciples to 'take my yoke upon you, and learn from me . . . For my yoke is easy, and my burden is light'. This is a reminder that it is God and not we ourselves who should determine the course of our life and the appropriate burdens we must shoulder.

The final part of the reply is that God's 'state/ Is kingly'. He has thousands of angelic servants who are able to communicate his messages to all places and all times unceasingly. The poet is not in fact the only mouthpiece of the divine, however much he feels called to be just that. The famous final line, 'They also serve who only stand and wait', is often taken to mean that passively enduring suffering – literally waiting around – is itself sufficient service. I wonder, though, whether the term 'wait' is stronger than that – waiting as a 'waiter' or servant does, close to the master or mistress, watching intently for instructions or new biddings. 'Waiting' for the Lord is in the psalms an image of intense and alert prayer (see Psalms 40.1; 62.5; 123.2). I believe that the poet is calling the frustrated political activist in himself to a life of greater contemplation.

Is there a significant constraint in your life that you have to be patient about? Pray for understanding of a calling appropriate to this stage of life.

Saturday

The problem, unstated till now, is how
to live in a damaged body
in a world where pain is meant to be gagged
uncured   un-grieved-over   The problem is
to connect, without hysteria, the pain
of any one's body with the pain of the body's world
For it is the body's world
they are trying to destroy forever
The best world is the body's world
filled with creatures   filled with dread
misshapen so   yet the best we have
our raft among the abstract worlds
and how I longed to live on this earth
walking her boundaries   never counting the cost

Adrienne Rich

This contemporary poem forms an interesting comparison and
contrast with Milton's sonnet 'On his blindness', though Rich's
poem is part of a longer sequence about the body and the world.
There is a kind of inner dialogue going on here too, about how to
'live in a damaged body', but the focus of concern and the param-
eters of belief are quite different. Rich's poem assumes no religious
framework, no existence of a God who will call us to account for
how our lives and talents are spent. Indeed, the poet suggests that
'the abstract worlds' (of which religion must be one) are something
we need protection from. Nevertheless, there is an urgency that is
reminiscent of the tone of Milton's poem, with its desire to be able

to affect things in the real world, from a perspective of now being impaired.

The poem begins with outlining a problem, 'unstated till now', and it is the problem of living with pain in a context where you are supposed to repress pain, and not to mention or lament suffering. It is hard to know whether the narrator of the poem is saying that she has not articulated the problem for herself before now, or that no one has done so. The impression is of someone who is accustomed to rehearse academic arguments, and is therefore claiming to be the first in the field to pose the dilemma explicitly. However, it is as if the tone of objective argument is pulled at by the always present undertow of chronic pain that the narrator is dealing with. This comes through in a sort of series of gasps, punctuated only by spaces (fighting for breath?): 'gagged/ uncured   un-grieved-over'. The term 'gagged' is strong, suggesting almost a kidnap situation. It is as if there is a reality – bodily pain – that is forbidden to speak.

The narrator puts the problem another way. It is how to connect individual bodily pain with 'the pain of the body's world', and to do so 'without hysteria'. Again, there is a tight-lipped concern to be objective. At one level, it is temptingly common, when in pain, for that almost to become one's whole world, for the world around to be experienced only through pain – the individual's pain. The narrator is striving to avoid being accused of this; rather she seeks to explain that her pain is putting her acutely in touch with a greater pain which is in fact currently occurring to 'the body's world', the material environment, this planet that we know only through our bodies. The hurting body can apprehend what the healthy body may be able to ignore, lost in abstractions, remote from awareness of its own vulnerability and bodiliness. The experience of pain is a profound dimension of knowledge that has been overlooked.

There follows a cry of lament for the body's world. This clearly relates to the material environment which is in danger of destruction from over-exploitation and climate change. But repeatedly calling this 'the body's world' keeps announcing the primacy of the vulnerable body as the touchstone for how the whole world is to be named, experienced and cherished. The narrator is aware of multiple versions of reality, competing theories or world-views – perhaps economic, nationalistic, or religious – that may justify all sorts of actual violent practice in the tender material world of human, animal and vegetable life. Again, there is a series of pained gasps as she names the reality of the latter: 'filled with creatures   filled with dread/ misshapen so   yet the best we have'.

For the body's world is 'our raft among the abstract worlds'. The term 'raft' is beautifully chosen to imply something both material and protective amid a dangerous and churning sea. Yet it is not very protective; it is a life-saver, but of the most basic and provisional kind, still leaving us open to the sky and uncertain about navigation. This concept is 'the best we have', the reality that must, urgently, be clung to if we are to survive at all.

The poem ends with an outburst of passionate longing, which brings together the narrator's current frustration with her (perhaps permanent) inability to roam the earth freely and her agony that the earth is threatened as it is. She laments that she cannot now herself walk without 'counting the cost', but, more profoundly, that no one can now experience their life on the planet, as older, more sustainable societies may have done, without 'costing the earth'.

Have you ever attended to or prayed for the life of the earth with the kind of urgency that is found in this poem? When you experience pain, do you allow it to isolate you from others or to make connections?

WEEK 5

'There are quite different things going on'
Altered perspectives

Monday

———————·•◆•·———————

The Kingdom

It's a long way off but inside it
There are quite different things going on:
Festivals at which the poor man
Is king and the consumptive is
Healed; mirrors in which the blind look
At themselves and love looks at them
Back; and industry is for mending
The bent bones and the minds fractured
By life. It's a long way off, but to get
There takes no time and admission
Is free, if you will purge yourself
Of desire, and present yourself with
Your need only and the simple offering
Of your faith, green as a leaf.

R. S. Thomas

It is the start of the last fortnight of Lent, and the beginning of Passiontide. Increasingly, we are entering a period, leading up to the memorial of Christ's crucifixion and resurrection, that is fraught with mystery. It is the time when we are mostly vividly brought to recall how, in St Paul's words, 'God chose what is foolish in the world to shame the wise; God chose what is weak in the world to shame the strong' (1 Corinthians 1.27).

The poems chosen for this week have in common the theme of reversals and altered perspectives. This poem addresses the idea of

God's 'kingdom' – the most important feature of Jesus' preaching during his ministry, and one of the conflictual areas around his trial and execution. In a political context where there were many actual rebellions against Roman colonial power and their Jewish governors, Jesus' teaching seems to have strayed dangerously close to presenting him as a rival political authority. Some of his followers as well as his enemies took it this way. But Jesus also undercut these expectations repeatedly, proposing a quite different sort of authority. The events of Passiontide seem to bear out this reversal of expectation.

The Gospels include many different images and parables about the nature of the kingdom he proclaimed, many of them contradictory or challenging. It will be like a great supper party, but none of the respectable people will end up as guests – just the riff-raff from the streets (Luke 14.15–24). It is both already among us, and yet it will only be revealed at the end of the ages. This poem by R. S. Thomas assumes a background understanding of Jesus' puzzling teaching about the 'kingdom', and builds on it.

As if beginning in the middle of a conversation or explanation (the word 'kingdom' is not used except in the title), the narrator announces it as being 'a long way off', but makes it clear that its nature is such as to defeat our normal way of constructing reality – 'There are quite different things going on'. He then lists some examples of these, and they remind us rather of the Beatitudes, that startling list of blessings that has never matched any political reality before or since, asserting that those who are truly blessed are the poor, the persecuted, the meek, those who weep and long for justice (Matthew 5.1–11).

One example of healing/reversal that is developed is the idea of the blind person being able to see again. Giving sight to the blind was a feature of Jesus' healing ministry, and was a highly symbolic aspect of Jewish prophecy about what would herald the presence of God's salvation (for example, Luke 7.22). But it is a double-edged idea in the Bible as 'blindness' is also frequently used as an image of the unconscious or deliberate refusal to see (for example, Isaiah 6.9–10). In this poem, the 'blind' are finally able to see themselves in a mirror, but when they do face themselves honestly, they find not that they are judged but that 'love looks at them/ Back'. It is reminiscent of Paul's famous chapter about love: 'For now we see in a mirror, dimly, but then we will see face to face' (1 Corinthians 13.12).

A fresh image that is used is the idea of what 'industry' is for in the kingdom of God. The word is carefully chosen to suggest not only individual endeavour but everything that is constructed and organized in human society for commercial gain. Rather than being for amassing capital (with scant concern for the cost to the humanity of workers, consumers or speculators involved), it is 'for mending/ The bent bones and the minds fractured/ By life.' R. S. Thomas' Welsh context had seen generations of miners whose bodies had been destroyed by their work. By such contrasts with society as we know it, the narrator fleshes out what 'a long way off' God's kingdom is for us.

However, with a repetition of this phrase he then insists that getting there 'takes no time and admission/ Is free' – a classic reversal rather like several of Jesus' sayings. This is clearly a matter of a profound shift of perspective and priority. The rest of the poem defines what 'free' means – rattled off in a casual way which at first glance sounds genuinely easy, simple and straightforward. But on closer inspection it turns out to involve, in T. S. Eliot's phrase, 'not less than everything'.

First, we have to purge ourselves of 'desire'. Given that we have had our identities constructed as consumers within a world where 'industry' in the sense of capital is king, that will involve shedding whatever we have previously been taught to want. Then, we have to present ourselves with our 'need only' – this is the genuine thing, rather than the induced 'desire'. To come with our need suggests that we have to give up our pride and any expectations that we can earn or deserve entry to the kingdom as a result of our own efforts or on our own merits. And finally, we are required to bring the 'simple offering' of our faith 'green as a leaf'. There is a fresh, child-like faith and trust that we have to bring with us, which may be difficult for those of us whom life has taught to be cynical and disappointed. But these simple, tough things are the entry requirements for the home we are seeking.

What kinds of desire do you need to 'purge' yourself of?

Tuesday

The Skylight

You were the one for skylights. I opposed
Cutting into the seasoned tongue-and-groove
Of pitch pine. I liked it low and closed,
Its claustrophobic, nest-up-in-the-roof
Effect. I liked the snuff-dry feeling,
The perfect, trunk-lid fit of the old ceiling.
Under there, it was all hutch and hatch.
The blue slates kept the heat like midnight thatch.

But when the slates came off, extravagant
Sky entered and held surprise wide open.
For days I felt like an inhabitant
Of that house where the man sick of the palsy
Was lowered through the roof, had his sins forgiven,
Was healed, took up his bed and walked away.

Seamus Heaney

This poem, which is part of a longer sequence, also assumes familiarity with the ministry of Jesus – specifically one of the most dramatic
of the healing miracles, the remarkable moment when the friends
of a paralysed man climb up onto the roof of the house where Jesus
is teaching, surrounded by crowds. Making a hole in the roof, they
lower their friend through on a stretcher to Jesus' feet so that he will
touch and cure him (Mark 2.1–12). Familiarity has perhaps meant
that readers of the biblical story no longer hear it as the very odd and
disturbing event it must have been.

The poem is constructed as one side of a conversation, which appears to be focusing on home improvements centred on the topmost room in a home – perhaps a bedroom or an attic study of some kind. The narrator presents himself as the one who was not really in favour of putting in a skylight, and there were clearly many good practical arguments for his position: it meant cutting into some skilful original work on the traditional tongue-and-groove ceiling; the initial fit was perfect, and working with the external slates; the roof as a whole was working efficiently to retain the heat indoors. But there is also a strong sense of his emotional opposition to the change proposed: he likes a low, closed ceiling; the word 'claustrophobic' is used positively because of the sense of 'nesting' somewhere safe and enclosed, as if tucked away in a trunk with a well-fitting lid. Even the dust is appreciated as 'snuff-dry'. We have the impression of someone hunkered down indoors where 'it was all hutch and hatch', with a resistance to being asked to let in the light or step outside a confined space that has become very cosy. It is beginning to sound as if the poem is about much more than home improvements.

This poem is a sonnet, with the theme or dilemma proposed in the first eight lines and then answered in the remaining six, and there is a strong contrast between the two parts insisted on here, between the line where the slates are still on, holding in the heat, and the line where they come off. There is a significant pause for breath before they do. It is interesting to note also how the tight, neat rhyme scheme of the first part of the poem dissolves into much looser half-rhymes as the poem (and the person who is the voice of the poem) opens up.

After the careful and cosy list of reasons why cutting out a skylight was to be feared, the event itself is described in a single sentence: 'extravagant/ Sky entered and held surprise wide open.' Everything prior to this has been described from the perspective of being inside the dark room, and the alteration is dramatic, not to say miraculous. 'Sky' itself entered, and the 'surprise' of his reaction is sustained – it is not possible to return to the closed attitude of his previous views on the subject.

The poem leaves us to fill in the blanks about what the surprise has done to him, simply comparing his feelings (whatever they are) to those of the people who lived in the house (whatever they were) – where suddenly their roof came off, a sick man entered from above and then was dramatically healed, departing with his stretcher over his shoulder. We are left to imagine the brickdust, the gaping hole in the roof, the sense of being 'broken into', the shock of being the hosts to a miracle performed on a complete stranger, the flooding in of the sunlight, and the impossibility of reconstructing their homely reality as it was before the event – in more ways than one.

So the poem refreshes our experience of the biblical story, by making the 'bricks and mortar' aspect of it vivid and concrete, by shifting our perspective from the man healed to the hapless hosts of the event, and by exploring a contemporary psyche, with whom we may identify, from within. The inbreaking of the 'kingdom' described in R. S. Thomas' poem may entail some real and shocking 'breaking in'.

Choose one of the Gospel miracle stories that is important to you, and read it slowly, thinking about the events from the point of view of a bystander.

Wednesday

Rublev

One day, God walked in, pale from the grey steppe,
slit-eyed against the wind, and stopped,
said, Colour me, breathe your blood into my mouth.

I said Here is the blood of all our people,
these are their bruises, blue and purple,
gold, brown, and pale green wash of death.

These (god) are the chromatic pains of flesh,
I said, I trust I make you blush,
O I shall stain you with the scars of birth

For ever. I shall root you in the wood,
under the sun shall bake you bread
of beechmast, never let you forth

to the white desert, to the starving sand.
But we shall sit and speak around
one table, share one food, one earth.

Rowan Williams

Andrei Rublev's icon showing the persons of the Trinity as angels seated at
a table dates from the fourteenth century and is in the Tretyakov Gallery,
Moscow.

The icon painted by Andrei Rublev in fourteenth-century Russia has become one of the most famous and loved religious images in the contemporary world. It seems to combine the sense of transcendent presence with a kind of intimacy and communion that strikes a chord with many people. It is based on the story of Abraham and Sarah (Genesis 18) who 'entertained angels unawares', offering hospitality in the desert to three strangers who subsequently spoke with the voice of God and promised them a son. Tradition has interpreted this story as a biblical reference to the three persons of the Trinity.

The icon depicts three angels who are identical in their facial features, though wearing different robes. They are seated around a table that looks a little like a low altar, and there is a communion chalice on it. They incline their heads towards each other, but leave a space at the centre of the icon, so that it is as if the person gazing at the image is being invited to draw closer and be seated at the table as well.

The role of the icon painter is a religious calling, and the intention is to create a 'window' for prayer, so that attention is drawn to God rather than to the painting itself or to the artist's skill. As if taking this function for granted, the poem envisages a direct conversation between the artist and God in the process of its creation. In a reversal of our expectations around this beautiful image, it is not a calm or cosily spiritual dialogue. Neither is the artist a submissive or surrendered partner in the matter – rather he challenges the deity head on.

It begins bluntly, with God simply walking into the icon painter's contemporary studio, and demanding to be depicted. He is described in human terms as affected by the weather and landscape: 'pale from the grey steppe,/ slit-eyed against the wind'. The language of God's demand is intentionally incarnational, as if the icon painter could create through his choice of colours an enfleshed version of the Godhead whose image could speak: 'Colour me, breathe your blood into my mouth.' The image almost imagines that the artist is required to give his own lifeblood to let his icon become God's mouthpiece.

The icon painter, however, seizes the initiative and replies rather in the tone of Job, who famously took issue with God about the existence of undeserved suffering (Job 24). Referring to the palette of colours he is going to use for the painting, he announces that they depict 'the blood of all our people'. The blue, purple, green of the painting are their 'bruises', the 'chromatic pains of flesh', the 'pale green wash of death'. His tone is critical, even lecturing. The bracketed reference 'god' is without its capital 'G', and sounds like an ironic courtesy, as he goes on to say, 'I trust I make you blush.' There is a nice double edge to this remark. Not only does it make clear that God must take responsibility for human suffering, but it repeats the theme of blood as it actually infuses the face that arrived 'pale from the grey steppe'.

He proceeds to make a statement that parallels the making of the icon with the mystery of the incarnation itself, and insists on the violence of that event, a violence to which all vulnerable human flesh is subject: 'O I shall stain you with the scars of birth/ For ever.' The image of God will be rooted in the wood of the icon, almost its prisoner. The God who is present in his studio will not be free to depart like the biblical triad of angels back into the desert, just as the God who took flesh in Jesus 'emptied himself . . . humbled himself and became obedient to the point of death' (Philippians 2.7, 8).

Only in the last two lines, when the pain of the world and the vulnerability involved both in the act of incarnation and in the act of painting an icon have been acknowledged, is the astonishing intimacy between the human and the divine celebrated: 'But we shall sit and speak around/ one table, share one food, one earth.'

The poem does not have a definite rhyme scheme, but there are half-rhymes and assonances that tie the lines together: 'steppe'/'stopped'; 'people'/'purple'; 'flesh'/'blush'. And at the end of each three-line stanza there is a half-rhyme using the sound 'th' – 'mouth', 'death', 'birth', 'forth', 'earth'. Not only are most of these words with primal meanings for human existence, but the work of pronouncing these words at the front of the mouth, using tongue and lips, reminds the reader of the sheer physicality of incarnation, or of being a mouthpiece for God.

So the reversals are many. This is not an icon of ethereal beauty depicting some bloodless or fantasy realm; it is wood and paint created in a real context by an artist of robust and challenging faith, which speaks of the God who, in answer to such faith, took human flesh and accepted human pain.

Spend time with a religious image that is important to you, and use it as a prompt to pray about the world.

Thursday

————◆•◆•————

Sheep Fair Day

'The real aim is not to see God in all things, it is that God, through us,
should see the things that we see.' Simone Weil

I took God with me to the sheep fair. I said, 'Look,
there's Liv, sitting on the wall, waiting;
these are pens, these are sheep,
this is their shit we are walking in, this is their fear.
See that man over there, stepping along the low walls
between pens, eyes always watching,
mouth always talking, he is the auctioneer.
That is wind in the ash trees above, that is sun
splashing us with running light and dark.
Those men over there, the ones with their faces sealed,
are buying or selling. Beyond in the ring
where the beasts pour in, huddle and rush,
the hoggets are auctioned in lots.
And that woman with the ruddy face and the home-cut hair
and a new child on her arm, that is how it is to be woman
with the milk running, sitting on wooden boards
in this shit-milky place of animals and birth and death
as the bidding rises and falls.'

Then I went back outside and found Fintan.
I showed God his hand as he sat on the rails,
how he let it trail down and his fingers played

107

in the curly back of a ewe. Fintan's a sheep-man
he's deep into sheep, though it's cattle he keeps now,
for sound commercial reasons.

                                      'Feel that,' I said,
'feel with my heart the force in that hand
that's twining her wool as he talks.'
Then I went with Fintan and Liv to Refreshments,
I let God sip tea, boiling hot, from a cup,
and I lent God my fingers to feel how it burned
when I tripped on a stone and it slopped.
'This is hurt,' I said, 'there'll be more.'
And the morning wore on and the sun climbed
and God felt how it is when I stand too long,
how the sickness rises, how the muscles burn.

Later, at the back end of the afternoon,
I went down to swim in the green slide of river,
I worked my way under the bridge, against the current,
then I showed how it is to turn onto your back
with, above you and a long way up, two gossiping pigeons,
and a clump of valerian, holding itself to the sky.
I remarked on the stone arch as I drifted through it,
how it dapples with sunlight from the water,
how the bridge hunkers down, crouching low in its track
and roars when a lorry drives over.

And later again, in the kitchen,
wrung out, at day's ending, and empty,
I showed how it feels
to undo yourself,
to dissolve, and grow age-old, nameless:

woman sweeping a floor, darkness growing.

                                              Kerry Hardie

This poem forms an interesting comparison with the previous one, as it also turns the tables on God and demands a hands-on understanding of human life as it is lived moment to moment in the body. It is based on taking seriously a saying of the modern mystic Simone Weil, which reverses a rather bland traditional religious injunction that we should attempt 'to see God in all things'. The starting point of this poem is that, rather, God should be invited, through us, to 'see the things that we see'. It is an arresting idea about the meaning of prayer, but very consistent with the determination of the icon painter in Rowan Williams' poem that God should feel in the flesh the pains as well as the beauty that we feel.

The narrator in this poem, therefore, decides to take God with her throughout her prosaic day attending a sheep fair in rural Ireland. The story is told in a matter of fact and conversational way, interspersing explanations about what the narrator did or saw, along with an internal running commentary to God about the nature and meaning of what she is seeing, what is being felt by various players, and what it means. She makes no assumptions that God has already seen or understood any of these things before, so the commentary is rather like what might be offered to a child ('See that man over there . . . he is the auctioneer'), or indeed to someone completely unfamiliar with our planet ('That is wind . . . that is sun'). As a result, the reader gets to see both familiar and unfamiliar aspects of her world in a new light.

The first section of the poem sets the scene. Sometimes the narrator offers lists that bracket physical items that can be observed or trodden in with emotions that can only be sensed – pens, sheep, the animals' shit but also their fear. The sense is that all these things are equally tangible, equally real parts of this event that God must experience. Sometimes there are acute visual observations of human behaviour and self-presentation that do not need further explaining. The auctioneer is the one with his 'eyes always watching,/ mouth always talking'; the buyers and sellers are 'the ones with their faces sealed'. This is a world where men are in charge and women are watching; yet it is as if the women are in touch with the whole picture (as God must learn to be) of what the scene means to all the creatures involved. The breastfeeding new mother with her 'ruddy face and the home-cut hair' is connected viscerally with the sheep being auctioned, 'with the milk running . . . in this shit-milky place of animals and birth and death'.

But the next section starts by focusing on the tenderness of a man – a one-time sheep farmer who is here because he loves sheep, but can't afford to farm them any more. This is shown to God through an intense focus on Fintan's hand as he idly fingers a ewe's back: 'feel with my heart the force in that hand/ that's twining her wool as he talks.' The poem moves on, rather like a hand-held camera, to record the next prosaic event, a slightly spilled cup of tea. The narrator uses the mild pain of her scalded fingers to make an ironic comment about human suffering overall: 'This is hurt,' I said, 'there'll be more.'

The poem has interspersed the description of the business scene with an awareness of the weather and the landscape, and this begins to assert itself more towards the end of the poem (as the narrator is getting tired and overheated in the sun). There is a final section – the dip in the river to cool off, which again offers God some startling perspectives on the physical world: the clump of valerian 'holding itself to the sky', the gossiping pigeons seen from below, and the sunlight dappling the underneath of a stone arch of the bridge she is floating under.

As the narrator signs off, 'wrung out, at day's ending, and empty', we are left with the powerful impression that the 'God' who has been asked to live an ordinary human day through her eyes, ears, intuitions, compassion and her tired but sensuous body has learned something.

Using this poem as a model, write a journal taking God through your typical day, highlighting what is most important for God to notice and understand.

Friday

Afterwards

The principalities, the powers, the politicians,
The ones who pose in the spotlight
Centre-stage, and magnetise us as they stalk
Towards bankruptcy, murder, betrayal, suicide,
And other traditional exits

The audience leaves, discussing nuances.
A scatter of sweet-papers, ash,
Smells hanging around behind. The audience leaves.

And in they come, rolling up their sleeves,
With hoovers and mops, buckets and brushes and Brasso,
Making it ready for the next time, nobody watching,
With small uncompetitive jokes, with backchat
About coach-trips, soaps, old men,
And a great sloshing of water.

This is where we ought to be. Not
Up on the stage with the rich and the Richards,
Rehearsing already their entrance for the next house,
The precise strut that registers power,

But down on our hands and knees,
Laughing, and mopping up.

U. A. Fanthorpe

This poem is a reflection on the experience of watching a performance of Shakespeare's *Richard III*, and then thinking about what happens 'afterwards' in the vacated auditorium. The meaning of a play is normally understood to be within the boundaries of the performance itself, and that is where our attention is directed; but the poet here is expanding the boundaries of meaning, and proposing that, in a reversal of perspective, we should focus instead on the moment when the cleaners arrive.

The poem begins with the characters whose drama we are supposed to watch and learn from. Their theme is power, and the repeated alliteration insists on this: 'The principalities, the powers, the politicians,/ The ones who pose'. As they seize the centre-stage, they mesmerize us – though no actual purposes are mentioned, only the list of dramatic and violent ends they may come to. And if you inspect these first few lines, you find that there is as yet no proper verb; it isn't a sentence and the punctuation trails away. It is as if the posturing of those on stage (or actually in power in our world) is all pose and no concrete action.

We switch to the audience who finally turn out to be the subject of the verb, with the power simply to 'leave' all that posturing behind by departing from the theatre. The audience are momentarily interested in what they have seen, abstractly 'discussing nuances', which nevertheless seem rather evanescent, compared with the reality of the prosaic mess they have left behind: 'A scatter of sweet-papers, ash,/ Smells hanging around'.

The audience has therefore departed when the next lot of significant characters makes their entrance. The cleaning women arrive with a spontaneous energy, 'rolling up their sleeves' to do the physical things that will make the next performance ready and the next audience comfortable. They have ordinary tools that do things: mops, brushes, polish. They take action unselfconsciously, 'nobody watching', rather than practise acting in a way that will draw attention to themselves. They slosh water rather than stalk around. Their conversation is humorous and uncompetitive, with an eye-rolling lack of respect for 'old men'. They are interested in getting done what needs doing, rather than seeking power.

As the narrator says, 'This is where we ought to be.' The whole poem is using the experience of what goes on in the whole of a theatre's world to ask us to notice what goes on in the real world, and to place ourselves and our focus with those who are normally unnoticed. This is where real action happens, rather than mere rehearsal. What passes for power is no more than a 'precise strut that registers power'.

As in Jesus' teaching about the reversals in the kingdom of God, 'many who are first will be last, and the last will be first' (Mark 10.31), and, 'whoever wishes to be first among you must be slave of all' (Mark 10.44). And there is a suggestion that such humility might actually be more fun, 'down on our hands and knees,/ Laughing, and mopping up.'

Unless this is something that you do all the time, volunteer for a job that involves clearing up after others, whether at home, at church or in the local community. Reflect on what you notice while you are doing it.

Saturday

The Donkey

When fishes flew and forests walked
    And figs grew upon thorn,
Some moment when the moon was blood
    Then surely I was born.

With monstrous head and sickening cry
    And ears like errant wings,
The devil's walking parody
    On all four-footed things.

The tattered outlaw of the earth,
    Of ancient crooked will;
Starve, scourge, deride me: I am dumb,
    I keep my secret still.

Fools! For I also had my hour;
    One far fierce hour and sweet:
There was a shout about my ears,
    And palms before my feet.

G. K. Chesterton

This poem, which used to be mandatory for children to learn by heart, is a classic of reversed perspectives. Unexpected prophecy in the mouth of a donkey is highly suitable for celebrating Palm Sunday, the festival of the king who rides humbly on an ass, rather than on a war horse like the Roman conquerors. We are reminded of another donkey who spoke in the Bible – Balaam's ass, who saw and responded to an angel while his master was oblivious (Numbers 22).

The poem is written with the donkey as narrator, and in a way never moves beyond that perspective. Much is implied about the person the ass carries, but Jesus is never mentioned – the reader supplies knowledge of the Palm Sunday story. The economic use of words and the tight rhyme scheme supply a deceptive simplicity.

In the first stanza he sets himself up as a kind of gruesome impossibility of nature, like fishes that fly, forests that walk or figs that grow on thorns. The walking forests sound rather Shakespearean, reminding us of Birnam wood, which did, in a fashion, 'come to Dunsinane' in *Macbeth*. The mood is about inevitable tragedy that is working towards its completion, as Palm Sunday leads towards the crucifixion. But the figs that grow on thorns sound biblical; it is a nonsense proverb – do figs grow upon thorns? (cf. Luke 6.44). And yet, in the Old Testament, figs stand for what is good, while thorns represent evil – may good yet come of evil? The blood-shot moon reminds us of the signs of the coming apocalypse predicted in the Bible (Revelation 6.12). If such a thing as this donkey can walk the earth, perhaps it is another sign of the time to come.

The second stanza stresses first the inelegant physique and cry of the beast, but represents ugliness as sinister – 'monstrous', 'sickening'. 'Errant wings' rather brilliantly suggests the large flapping ears of the donkey, but there are undertones of evil, as if this is a fallen angel from hell – one who had wings who went wrong. The creature is 'The devil's walking parody'; he is not funny.

In the third stanza, he refers to himself as 'The tattered outlaw of the earth' almost as if he were the traditional biblical 'scapegoat', the animal who was sent out into the desert to die, ritually carrying on his back the sins of the people. This reminds us of the role that Jesus himself takes as the Suffering Servant (Isaiah 53); the invocation to 'Starve, scourge, deride me: I am dumb' prophetically recalls the silence that Jesus will preserve at his trial and flagellation.

Finally, he rounds on those who have become convinced that the donkey is ludicrous, or monstrous, or a harbinger of evil, with a triumphant cry: 'Fools!' It is those who think conventionally about power who turn out to be the foolish ones who cannot see the reversals that God's kingdom brings. And the last lines take us away from self-contempt, just showing us a hint of the Palm Sunday event from the perspective of a beast of burden who plods along, doing what needs doing, and yet actually carrying the Saviour: 'There was a shout about my ears,/ And palms before my feet.'

Have you ever, however unexpectedly, 'had your hour'?

WEEK 6

'Love's austere and lonely offices'
Holy Week

Monday

————◆————

Those Winter Sundays

Sundays too my father got up early
and put his clothes on in the blueblack cold,
then with cracked hands that ached
from labor in the weekday weather made
banked fires blaze. No one ever thanked him.

I'd wake and hear the cold splintering, breaking.
When the rooms were warm, he'd call,
and slowly I would rise and dress,
fearing the chronic angers of that house,

Speaking indifferently to him,
who had driven out the cold
and polished my good shoes as well.
What did I know, what did I know
of love's austere and lonely offices?

Robert Hayden

This is Holy Week, when we reflect on the mystery of 'love's austere and lonely offices' enacted on behalf of all humankind. The poem that starts the week is not a religious poem, but it speaks of the human love that makes daily self-sacrifice possible – and of how that sacrifice may first be ignored, but later remembered as symbolizing the heart of a relationship.

The narrator's voice comes through, first as childhood memory and then as a reflective adult, recalling what his father did for him. The setting is getting up on a Sunday to go to church in best clothes and shoes. Sunday was the only day of rest, and the only possible morning when a working man could lie in bed. But the first words of the poem announce his father's self-sacrifice: 'Sundays too my father got up early'. That simple 'too' implies years of getting out of bed into the perishing cold, day after day without respite, to go out and labour in all weathers with 'cracked hands'. And the poignant, bleak comment: 'No one ever thanked him.'

Perhaps it is only readers who remember what houses were like in winter before the advent of central heating who quite appreciate what his father did. There was no way of getting up into a warm house unless someone got up first in the cold, and tried to resurrect the fires that had been 'banked' with coal dust the night before. If the fires had completely gone out they had to clean out the fireplaces (a filthy job), and start again to light fires. Bedrooms and clothes were icy on winter mornings. Your hands got cracked not just from manual labour and dirty housework but from chilblains. You longed to stay under the blankets until it was warm.

The second stanza speaks of how the cold was 'splintering, breaking'. This actually refers to the way coal splits and spits as it is catching fire and becoming hotter, but the implication is that the cold is being defeated and destroyed, the evil power of the cold winter being taken on and broken by this sacrificial work. The narrator recalls dressing slowly (this was a luxury only possible because the edge had been taken off the cold). There is an implied reluctance to go downstairs, 'fearing the chronic angers of that house'. We are given no information about what the 'angers' refer to, just as we know nothing about other family members, including the child's mother. Perhaps the unusual willingness of the father to get up and do a 'woman's work' suggests that he was trying to win her love in an atmosphere of unhappiness. Perhaps he was despised for being only a manual labourer.

In the last stanza, the narrator judges his behaviour as a child (or perhaps a teenager), 'Speaking indifferently to him'. His father now seems like a brave hero 'who had driven out the cold' but also as an attentive daddy with an eye for detail who had 'polished my good shoes as well' in preparation for church. But the final two lines convey not just retrospective guilt but a wealth of subsequent hard-earned wisdom acquired over the years between then and now: 'What did I know, what did I know/ of love's austere and lonely offices?'

No doubt the narrator himself (as well as the reader) has by now stood on the other side in a relationship where one is doing all the giving and the other is apparently oblivious. But as we think of Jesus moving towards his death, among followers who will misunderstand him and desert him at the point of crisis, the lines can stand as our cry from the heart as his disciples.

Who in your life has made sacrifices for you out of love? And for whom have you willingly made sacrifices?

Tuesday

———•—•———

Fire and Ice

Some say the world will end in fire,
Some say in ice.
From what I've tasted of desire
I hold with those who favour fire.
But if it had to perish twice,
I think I know enough of hate
To say that for destruction ice
Is also great
And would suffice.

Robert Frost

This famous poem, of deceptive simplicity, is not a straightforwardly religious poem. But its insights are relevant to the passions and destructive impulses of the events of Holy Week, as Jesus engages in controversy with his enemies in Jerusalem, with the prospect of death ahead of him.

It's a witty poem and the impulse is to laugh when you first hear it. However, it lingers in the mind and becomes much more sinister than funny on further reflection. The tone is first conversational, then bitter. The jolting, repeated end-rhymes help to make the poem amusing, but also bring great emphasis to certain hugely destructive ideas.

The poem begins by apparently contrasting two contemporary scientific theories about the future of the planet over aeons of time – is it gradually getting warmer, or will the earth perish eventually in another global ice age? But there are other undercurrents, since the speculations might equally well be about the nature of the afterlife, specifically the nature of hell.

The next two lines definitely wrench the references away from neutral scientific theories into the personal hell that can be experienced as a result of disappointed or betrayed feelings: 'From what I've tasted of desire/ I hold with those who favour fire.' The narrator conveys his bitterness by ironically still using the moderate phrases of academic debate ('I hold with those who favour'), as if this was still an objective enquiry.

With an equally objective tone, he then posits – as if it potentially made any sort of sense – an absurdity: 'But if it had to perish twice'. Then he lapses again into the personal knowledge that underlies the poem: 'I think I know enough of hate', before once again positing an ironic, moderately phrased proposition about its destructive power, which 'would suffice'. This tight-lipped statement with the understated word (which nevertheless rhymes savagely with 'ice') implies massive repressed anger.

The overall implication is that the experience of burning, thwarted desire has turned to an all-consuming hatred. Just as the narrator's world has ended because of disappointment in desire, so his subsequent icy fury will be sufficient to destroy another's world. His own capacity for compassion or forgiveness is frozen beyond recall. The poem may begin to remind us of Dante's vision of hell. In the seventh circle the violent are punished with fire; in the ninth (and deepest) circle are the traitors like Judas, who are depicted as frozen in ice.

What began as a piece of witticism has turned into a carefully honed exploration of how humans destroy and betray one another. The implied personal experience on which the poem is based suggests a much more worldwide application of this anatomy of sin.

How much do you know about your own capacity for hatred or cruelty?

Wednesday

I am the great sun

From a Normandy crucifix of 1632

I am the great sun, but you do not see me,
    I am your husband, but you turn away.
I am the captive, but you do not free me,
    I am the captain you will not obey.

I am the truth, but you will not believe me,
    I am the city where you will not stay.
I am your wife, your child, but you will leave me,
    I am that God to whom you will not pray.

I am your counsel, but you do not hear me,
    I am your lover whom you will betray,
I am the victor, but you do not cheer me,
    I am the holy dove whom you will slay.

I am your life, but if you will not name me,
Seal up your soul with tears, and never blame me.

Charles Causley

This poem was written in the twentieth century but it has the feel of a much older text. Causley, a Cornish poet, draws on ballad forms rather like the visionary poet William Blake. It has such apparent simplicity that it takes a while to notice that it is also in the form of a sonnet, this time the so-called Shakespearean sonnet which ends with a rhyming couplet after twelve lines of development. But this poem has roots that go back to much earlier traditions.

One of the ancient liturgical traditions associated with Holy Week is the 'Reproaches', a series of biddings spoken as if in the voice of God addressing his people. God draws attention to all the loving acts of creation and salvation undertaken for humankind, and contrasts them with the cruelty and rejection that humans have meted out to their saviour in return. The image of the saviour as the passionate lover of humanity who is then betrayed is a common theme in medieval spirituality, which finds expression in ballads and carols like 'Tomorrow shall be my dancing day'. By giving a poignant voice to a vulnerable, loving God who does not enforce our obedience, who suffers on our behalf, and must endure our rejection, the intention is that those who hear this kind of poetry should be moved to compassion and devotion in return.

The other major reference for this poem is St John's Gospel, in which Jesus announces his true identity in a series of 'I am' statements, such as, 'I am the bread of life' (John 6.35). In their turn, these claims (shown to be deeply resisted by the religious powers of his time) recall the sacred circumlocution for the name of God: 'I AM WHO I AM' (Exodus 3.14).

The poem deals with that profound resistance to seeing what is going on, which has been explored in a number of the poems in this book. The first stanza announces a paradox that has a serious double entendre underlying it. God is identified with the 'great sun', the source of light for humanity, by which we see everything that we can see – yet we do not notice it. Even the pagan world could see and respond to the life-giving sun that lights and warms the earth. But spoken aloud, the poem irresistibly recalls 'the great Son', the second person of the Trinity, identified with the Godhead, present with humanity, but whose 'own people did not accept him' (John 1.11).

But the divine narrator immediately proceeds to offer a whole list of different 'I am' metaphors – roles that ask for a response of different kinds, but each of which is resisted. 'I am your husband' – this recalls the Old Testament image of the covenant God as the husband of an unfaithful wife, who pleads with her and tries to woo her back to a honeymoon period (Hosea 2.14–23). 'I am the captive' – this echoes many biblical passages where the liberation of the captives is a symbol of the presence of God, but places God as the captive looking for us to help, as in Matthew 25. Then, with wordplay on the similar sounds of 'captive' and 'captain', the metaphor switches again – we will neither assist the vulnerable God nor obey the powerful one.

'I am the truth' echoes John's Gospel (John 14.6), and the corollary 'but you will not believe me' is a summary of the common response of those who opposed Jesus. The force of this statement is that it is, however, addressed to believers, or those of us who think we are. 'I am the city' recalls Jerusalem – either the actual place that Jesus wept over, whose downfall he predicted (Luke 19.41), or the 'holy city' of the book of Revelation, the place where God dwells with his people (Revelation 21.2). 'I am your wife, your child, but you will leave me' – the image of God as wife or child is arresting because it is not traditional to depict God in this way. However, this bidding follows very naturally in this ever-shifting series, and so it is provocative in a traditional way, even if earlier writers might not actually have used this imagery. Significantly it is at this point of shocking intimacy and betrayal that God explicitly reveals, 'I am that God to whom you will not pray.' This is a blunt challenge to every believer whose devotion is faltering.

The series continues – the counsel (lawyer or advocate) whom we will not listen to, the lover whom we will betray. Again there is a sense of shock to hear the word 'lover' applied to God; but this is very much the medieval image – itself dependent on the Song of Songs – coming to the fore and surprising modern sensibilities. 'I am the victor, but you do not cheer me' – this image recalls the time that Jesus answers his critics who want him to quell the enthusiasm of his disciples and the crowd as he enters Jerusalem. He announces that if the disciples keep silent, 'the stones would shout out' (Luke 19.40). The 'holy dove' refers to the traditional image of the Holy Spirit, who is the source of insight and truth but whom we resist. It is said that the sin against the Holy Spirit is the one that cannot be forgiven – to call good evil, and evil things good.

The final couplet locates responsibility back with the hearer – to agree to 'name' the God who finds endless ways to appeal to our love, or to repress our compassionate tears and thus deny the very source of our life.

The poem reads like an appeal for an internal spiritual response, but because of the plethora of images for God we have been made aware of the world outside our selfish egos – people close to us or with a claim on us for liberation, places where we should belong, truths we should recognize, and the consequences of our refusal to respond to the offer of salvation. The drama is set in the soul of the hearer, but the appeal of God encompasses our involvement in the sin of a violent and cold-hearted world.

Which of the 'I am' statements in this poem do you find most arresting? Why is that?

Maundy Thursday

Love

Love bade me welcome; yet my soul drew back,
    Guilty of dust and sin.
But quick-eyed Love, observing me grow slack
    From my first entrance in,
Drew nearer to me, sweetly questioning,
    If I lack'd any thing.

A guest, I answer'd, worthy to be here:
    Love said, You shall be he.
I the unkind, ungrateful? Ah, my dear,
    I cannot look on thee.
Love took my hand, and smiling did reply,
    Who made the eyes but I?

Truth, Lord, but I have marr'd them: let my shame
    Go where it doth deserve.
And know you not, says Love, who bore the blame?
    My dear, then I will serve.
You must sit down, says Love, and taste my meat:
    So I did sit and eat.

George Herbert

Maundy Thursday is the day when the Church commemorates the institution of the Eucharist, recalling the night when Jesus ate his last supper with his disciples before his arrest and trial. He took bread and wine and shared them, saying, 'This is my body that is for you ... This cup is the new covenant in my blood' (1 Corinthians 11.24–25). Since the very earliest times, Christians have gathered to retell the story and share bread and wine in memory of him.

This profound and continually available intimacy with the crucified saviour underlies Herbert's famous poem, although the elements of Holy Communion are not specifically mentioned. The poem also recalls various parables Jesus told about great feasts. One is the great feast where the invited guests failed to show up, and those who end up at the party are those who would least have expected to be there (Luke 14.15–24). Another is the prodigal son, who eventually returns to his father's house having claimed his inheritance ahead of time and then wasted it all. The guilty son resolves to ask to be forgiven but then to be treated as a servant, but his father welcomes him home without reserve and takes him aback by arranging a feast in his honour (Luke 15.11–32).

The first stanza sets a scene that is one of a guest arriving at a party, the host (personified Love) there on the doorstep to welcome the narrator soul immediately. But the see-saw dynamic of the poem (Love actively offering something, the narrator hesitating or withdrawing out of guilt) is announced in the first line: 'Love bade me welcome; yet my soul drew back'. Love, like a particularly attentive host or hostess, notices the reluctance and asks if the guest needs anything that has been overlooked. But there is a double entendre. Love puts the question 'observing me grow slack' – this is apparently about a shy guest's reluctance to enter a gracious home, but it could also imply that the soul has become 'slack' about personal devotion or attendance at Holy Communion, that 'means of grace'.

The second stanza has the soul and Love engage in a debate that is almost elegantly flirtatious in tone, yet completely serious in intent. The soul sees itself not as lacking some minor courtesy but as being himself completely lacking in worth – like the returning prodigal, he feels that he does not deserve to be treated as a guest. Told that he shall be worthy, he again denies this, as he is 'unkind, ungrateful' (like those who are the subject of God's accusations in Causley's poem, see p. 124). He asserts, 'I cannot look on thee.' The suggestion is that he is embarrassed to look his host in the face; but the underlying reference is to the terrifying prospect of looking directly at God.

Traditionally, to turn one's eyes directly upon God is to risk death. But the use of the endearment 'my dear', rather than 'my Lord', suggests that the reluctant soul does in fact want to draw closer. Continuing the gently romantic tone, Love takes his hand, smiles (is the narrator beginning to look at Love's face or does he just hear the smile in Love's voice?) and points out that he, the author of all creation, is the one who made the soul's eyes and therefore allows them to look at him without hurt.

In the final stanza, full of shame that will not depart, the soul is still arguing that his sins deny him the right – 'I have marr'd them'. He has used his eyes for sinful purposes and desires, instead of preserving the 'single eye' of faith, or being among the 'pure in heart' who will 'see God' (Matthew 5.8). Again, Love gently reproves him, not denying the reality of his sin and shame but reminding him 'who bore the blame' for his salvation. The soul, again with the telling endearment, offers to serve like the returning prodigal. Finally, Love ceases to cajole and offer and becomes like an insistent host, since nothing else, it appears, is going to puncture this soul's relentless self-deprecation: 'You must sit down, says Love, and taste my meat'. Again there is the double entendre – the 'meat' of the elegant imagined banquet: the 'meat' that is the flesh and blood of the saviour.

The last line, which is just six one-syllable words, has a force that derives from all the previous backward and forward arguing and reluctance. The soul finally takes action and agrees to receive and be fed. In just the same way, we have no doubt found every kind of excuse over the years not to come into God's presence, and not to receive communion. The apparently humble reasons we produce for not doing so turn out to be just another form of pride and resistance. We just need to do it.

How easy or hard do you find it to receive love or grace? Reflect on this as you attend a communion service.

Good Friday

Good Friday, 1613. Riding Westward

Let man's soul be a sphere, and then, in this,
The intelligence that moves, devotion is,
And as the other Spheres, by being grown
Subject to foreign motions, lose their own,
And being by others hurried every day,
Scarce in a year their natural form obey:
Pleasure or business, so, our souls admit
For their first mover, and are whirl'd by it.
Hence is't, that I am carried towards the west
This day, when my soul's form bends towards the east.
There I should see a sun, by rising set,
And by that setting endless day beget;
But that Christ on this cross, did rise and fall,
Sin had eternally benighted all.
Yet dare I almost be glad, I do not see
That spectacle of too much weight for me.
Who sees God's face, that is self life, must die;
What a death were it then to see God die?
It made his own lieutenant, Nature, shrink,
It made his footstool crack, and the sun wink.
Could I behold those hands which span the poles,
And turn all spheres at once, pierc'd with those holes?
Could I behold that endless height which is
Zenith to us, and our Antipodes,
Humbled below us? or that blood which is
The seat of all our souls, if not of his,
Made dirt of dust, or that flesh which was worn

By God, for his apparel, ragg'd and torn?
If on these things I durst not look, durst I
Upon his miserable mother cast mine eye,
Who was God's partner here, and furnish'd thus
Half of that sacrifice, which ransom'd us?
Though these things, as I ride, be from mine eye,
They are yet present to my memory,
For that looks towards them; and thou look'st towards me,
O Saviour as thou hang'st upon the tree;
I turn my back to thee, but to receive
Corrections, till thy mercies bid thee leave.
O think me worth thine anger, punish me,
Burn off my rusts, and my deformity,
Restore thine image, so much, by thy grace,
That thou may'st know me, and I'll turn my face.

John Donne

Although there are several profound Good Friday hymns, it is hard to find a reflective poem about the crucifixion that feels adequate, without resorting to a depiction that almost luxuriates in the details of torture. Such poems were rather popular in the late Middle Ages, and in our own generation some cinematic retellings of the story have fallen into the same trap, leaving the viewer either scoured by the violence or else rather exhilarated by it.

This seventeenth-century poem by Donne works well, precisely because of its restraint. It is about not looking directly at the cross, but recalling it while averting one's eyes. Rather than attempting to immerse the reader in the scenes at Golgotha, the focus of the poem keeps moving between that place, the mind and heart of the contemporary narrator, and the impact of the cross on the whole of the created cosmos. However, the opening ideas may feel like a bit of a struggle for a modern reader.

The title announces the contemporary context for the meditation – 'Riding Westward' – that is, facing away from the city of Jerusalem on Good Friday, a day when all Christian hearts should be turning towards it. Donne was among the group of poets known as the 'metaphysicals', who typically use a complex idea, theory or 'conceit' as the controlling image or starting place for their poetry. He starts by explaining why 'I am carried towards the west/ This day, when my soul's form bends towards the east.' His physical body is being transported on horseback in one direction, while his true self (the Platonic 'form' of his soul) is bending and yearning in the opposite direction. The image he uses is based on the current astronomical theory of the universe, which was imagined as a series of nested spheres containing the various heavenly bodies. It was thought that each sphere turned independently of the others, and was moved by its own 'intelligence'. However, this earth-centric model was beginning to be contested. It had been noted that the movement of a planet, unlike the stars, was erratic, and the reasons for this were a matter for contemporary debate. It could be 'Subject to foreign motions'. Thus, a planet might only occasionally ('Scarce in a year') obey its 'natural' path through the heavens.

Donne compares this observation with our own erratic religious devotion, which so seldom follows its proper path. Instead, because we allow other things to become our 'first mover', our souls are pulled out of true on a daily basis by 'Pleasure or business' instead, 'and are whirl'd by it'. This observation reminds us of Denise Levertov's poem about Adam, who ignores the hand of God, mesmerized by 'the whirling rides' (p. 10).

The narrator starts to envisage what he would be seeing if he were looking in the right direction, and experiments with the idea of sunrise, sunset, the rising of the Son through the acceptance of death, the prospective death of the sun to all sinners had not the Son risen. Through dazzling double and triple entendres, the poet implies the endless mystery of the crucifixion, and then returns to the fragile feelings of the narrator, who admits that it is a relief to be facing away from 'That spectacle of too much weight for me'. Again we have the tradition that to look at God's face is to risk death; what then if we witnessed God's death?

The idea is developed, using the traditional unimaginable paradoxes of the incarnation. He draws in once again the idea of the spheres, and who it is that really maintains the universe in motion:

'Could I behold those hands which span the poles,/ And turn all spheres at once, pierc'd with those holes?' Calling up these cosmic images and finding himself unequal to contemplate them, he turns to Mary at the foot of the cross, 'his miserable mother'. Yet that sight too is unbearable. Mary is seen not only as an agonized human mother, but as the majestic figure whose role in the incarnation provided 'Half of that sacrifice, which ransom'd us'.

Sustaining the image of being turned away, the narrator now feels the gaze of the crucified Christ on his back as he travels. He now embraces this idea as offering his back for punishment – punishment envisaged as a corrective burning away of flaws. There is something both poignant and deeply passionate about the appeal, 'O think me worth thine anger'. Although to modern ears it sounds almost masochistic, it has a pride within it, and a longing to be burnished and restored to the image of God that he was created to be, to be known and recognized.

After a long and convoluted poem, with complex explanations as to why he is travelling in the wrong direction, the last few words have the same simplicity and force as the end Herbert's poem, where the narrator finally agrees to receive the offered grace: 'I'll turn my face.'

Do you feel that you are travelling in the right direction in your life? If not, what could persuade you to turn your face?

Holy Saturday

───── ✦ ─────

Ikon: The Harrowing of Hell

Down through the tomb's inward arch
He has shouldered out into Limbo
to gather them, dazed, from dreamless slumber:
the merciful dead, the prophets,
the innocents just His own age and those
unnumbered others waiting here
unaware, in an endless void He is ending
now, stooping to tug at their hands,
to pull them from their sarcophagi,
dazzled, almost unwilling. Didmas,
neighbor in death, Golgotha dust
still streaked on the dried sweat of his body
no one had washed and anointed, is here,
for sequence is not known in Limbo;
the promise, given from cross to cross
at noon, arches beyond sunset and dawn.
All these He will swiftly lead
to the Paradise road: they are safe.
That done, there must take place that struggle
no human presumes to picture:
living, dying, descending to rescue the just
from shadow, were lesser travails
than this: to break
through earth and stone of the faithless world
back to the cold sepulchre, tearstained
stifling shroud; to break from *them*
back into breath and heartbeat, and walk

the world again, closed into days and weeks again,
wounds of His anguish open, and Spirit
streaming through every cell of flesh
so that if mortal sight could bear
to perceive it, it would be seen
His mortal flesh was lit from within, now,
and aching for home. He must return,
first, in Divine patience, and know
hunger again, and give
to humble friends the joy
of giving Him food – fish and a honeycomb.

Denise Levertov

Holy Saturday is often experienced, by those who are observing the liturgical 'triduum', the days from the evening of Maundy Thursday to the morning of the resurrection on Easter Sunday, as a day of limbo or vacancy. No services are usually held; it is a day of waiting upon the action of God in raising Christ from the dead. Ancient Christian tradition (incorporated into the Apostles' Creed) taught that Christ, between his death and resurrection, 'descended into hell', broke its power and redeemed from there all the righteous and faithful souls who had lived and died before his time (1 Peter 3.18–22). This is called the 'harrowing' (plundering) of hell.

The harrowing of hell is a favourite theme for much medieval illustration and drama, and also for the icon tradition in the Orthodox Church. Many Christians find it a helpful image of the way in which the work of Christ through the power of the cross and resurrection is able to reach and redeem every part of our selves and our world, even those aspects that may be hidden or long buried – all may step into the light of salvation. Past, present and future are all one, and all redeemed through the overwhelming power of God's grace.

Levertov here writes as if gazing at a particular icon of the event, and (rather as the artist Stanley Spencer does in his resurrection images) imagines in a concrete way what it was like for people to be hauled out from hell or limbo – and then what it was like for Christ to return into the world of his disciples in his resurrection body. In so doing she offers a fascinating angle on the meaning of the incarnation.

The poem starts with a journey 'down' from the tomb, but through the 'inward arch' rather than the resurrection movement which will involve rolling away the entrance stone and breaking out. There is an immediate sense of Christ's physical power ('He has shouldered out'), freeing souls almost like a parent with sleepy or reluctant children ('stooping to tug at their hands'), and his swift competence ('they are safe'). It is interesting who among the sequence of 'merciful dead' the poet picks out. The prophets are generically there, but she highlights not the famous figures of the Old Testament but those who were part of Jesus' own human story: the 'innocents just His own age' (the children slain by Herod's soldiers when Jesus' family fled to Egypt – they were, of course, his exact and overlooked peer group); Didmas the penitent thief, whom Jesus promised from the cross 'today you will be with me in Paradise' (Luke 23.43). The description of Didmas' unwashed, unanointed body recalls indirectly Christ's own experience of crucifixion but also points forward to the moment when the women will return with extra spices and encounter the mystery of the empty tomb.

The harrowing of hell is done and finished with, only halfway through the poem, as the second major subject begins to emerge. It is as if this day, Holy Saturday, is a pivotal moment that the poem itself mirrors in its two halves.

Dismissing all of Jesus' previous work (life, crucifixion, descent into hell) as 'lesser travails/ than this', the narrator announces the true struggle that is involved in undergoing bodily resurrection in order to 'walk/ the world again'. She describes the extraordinary movement back, stressing the concrete physical details that must be reinhabited, with consequent diminishment and self-limitation: earth and stone; cold sepulchre; 'tearstained/ stifling shroud'. It is like undergoing a second incarnation, but this time in full knowledge of the exact cost of that, returning to its betrayal by friends, its coldness and griefs, the limits and hungers of the body – at a moment when all his being is 'aching for home', for its limitless union with God. Instead, with

'Divine patience', he accepts once again 'breath and heartbeat', and being once more subject to the boundaries of time.

It is a tender and original meditation on the nature of incarnation itself, fleshing out the ancient Christian hymn found in St Paul's letter to the Philippians, which celebrates 'Christ Jesus, who, though he was in the form of God, did not regard equality with God as something to be exploited, but emptied himself' (Philippians 2.5–7). Charles Wesley's famous hymn speaks of a God who 'emptied himself of all but love', and the ending of the poem could be an icon of this. The poet recalls the resurrection narrative where Jesus asks for food (Luke 24.36–42): his love is shown in once more experiencing hunger and letting his friends meet his need. This is a God made manifest in vulnerability and not in power. Hell is plundered by the powerful saviour: friends of earth are reached through ordinary human neediness.

Read Philippians 2.5–11, the most ancient hymn to the incarnation, and use it as a meditation.

WEEK 7

'Never turning away again'

Resurrection

Easter Monday

---

i thank You God for most this amazing
day:for the leaping greenly spirits of trees
and a blue true dream of sky;and for everything
which is natural which is infinite which is yes

(i who have died am alive again today,
and this is the sun's birthday;this is the birth
day of life and of love and wings:and of the gay
great happening illimitably earth)

how should tasting touching hearing seeing
breathing any – lifted from the no
of all nothing – human merely being
doubt unimaginable You?

(now the ears of my ears awake and
now the eyes of my eyes are opened)

E. E. Cummings

While it is not explicitly a poem about the resurrection, it is hard to read this exuberant text without having the sense that it is hinting at an event that has erupted within the wholly natural world of the earth and sky and human senses, yet is somehow beyond the natural. As such, the wild (or absent) punctuation and bizarre word order that is characteristic of E. E. Cummings' poetry seem completely appropriate. This is an event that demands to be described and celebrated, yet it strains and cracks open ordinary human language.

Basically, this is a hymn of praise and thanksgiving, moving to a strong affirmation of faith in God. Made in the familiar shape of a sonnet, with three quatrains and a couplet, it is actually more structured than it initially seems, although the words struggle breathlessly to fit in. If spoken aloud, the poem wants to race along past its line endings, from the initial 'i' to the 'unimaginable You'.

The first stanza announces the theme of celebrating the day, with the word 'day' placed after the first line ending to explosive effect. Unusual word order is introduced straight away: 'most this amazing' ensures that the emphasis comes on 'most' rather than 'this'; 'blue true dream' makes us think not only that the sky is an intense colour but that a dream has come true; 'leaping greenly spirits of trees' means that we are conscious first of the extraordinary movement before we know that it applies to trees. Everything is super-vivid, alive beyond its own usual boundaries. Everything is both 'natural' and 'infinite'. The whole world is 'yes' – affirming, positive, responding to God, alive.

The second quatrain is completely enclosed in a bracket. (Brackets in Cummings' work often contain hugely important truths; this is hardly a stage whisper or a casual aside.) The first line could be either a strong statement of personal recovery from despair, or a resurrection announcement in the mouth of Christ, and the second line continues in the same tone. The 'sun's birthday' may refer to the equinox, where the day length begins to exceed the length of the hours of darkness; it may also suggest the divine Son who is also called 'Sun of righteousness'. Or it may be just a way of expressing how 'newborn' is the narrator's sense of delight: for 'life', 'love' and 'wings' are all also born today. The 'wings' (an odd member of the sequence) suggest that joy has a capacity to soar; and along with the 'blue true' sky, the 'leaping greenly' trees and the 'gay . . . earth' suggests the newly fledged qualities of the springtime. 'Happening illimitably' is another phrase like 'leaping greenly' – a verb and adverb placed together to qualify the noun that follows. The earth is defined as a place of limitless, seething activity.

The third stanza is an extraordinary confession of faith as a response to this vibrant, joyful world. Missing out all the adjectival words, this says: 'how should . . . any . . . human . . . being doubt . . . You?' But within those spaces are stuffed all the active human senses: 'tasting touching hearing seeing/ breathing' and the sense of salvation 'lifted from the no/ of all nothing' (which is the opposite of 'everything . . . which is yes'). And we have the contrast between the 'human merely being' and the 'unimaginable You'. The triumphant question reminds us of Psalm 8, 'What are human beings that you are mindful of them?'

The final two lines are also bracketed, and are like a comment on the whole poem, with its sudden, overwhelming sense of joy. The 'ears of my ears' that awake and the 'eyes of my eyes' that are opened suggest a listening and a looking that go beyond what is natural (they are both natural and infinite). There is a strong echo of the many biblical references to ears being blocked and eyes dimmed where humans resist responding to God, and correspondingly opened when the divine reality is made manifest. There is always a human choice about whether to notice what is before us: 'Let anyone with ears to hear listen' (Mark 4.9).

Think of a time when you have been 'surprised by joy'.

Tuesday

Food for risen bodies – II

On that final night, his meal was formal:
lamb with bitter leaves of endive, chervil,
bread with olive oil and jars of wine.

Now on Tiberias' shores he grills
a carp and catfish breakfast on a charcoal fire.
This is not hunger, this is resurrection:

he eats because he can, and wants to
taste the scales, the moist flakes of the sea,
to rub the salt into his wounds.

Michael Symmons Roberts

This poem starts where 'Ikon: The Harrowing of Hell' ends – with the risen Jesus sharing food with his disciples, this time according to the narrative in John's Gospel chapter 21. But it announces a very different perspective on Jesus' resurrection body. Whereas Levertov's poem sees the resurrection as a costly new process of incarnation, this one exults in the renewal of bodily sensations.

The poem reminds us how significant the process of sharing food with his friends has been in Jesus' life, and therefore how appropriate it is that the resurrection is also celebrated by a kind of feast. First, it points back to the setting for the last supper held the evening before Jesus' trial. It was a formal occasion because it was a Passover Seder meal, in which the different elements (even before Jesus blessed the bread and wine) would have had a traditional ritual meaning. The roast lamb was specifically slaughtered for the Passover feast, in memory of the meal held by the Israelites on the night that they were released from their slavery in Egypt (Exodus 12). The 'bitter leaves of endive' were prescribed to accompany the meal, to symbolize the bitter suffering during their time of slavery. Jesus was using the retelling of the story of deliverance as the background for his eucharistic instruction to bless and share bread and wine 'in remembrance of me' (Luke 22.14–20).

The second stanza speaks of the barbecue breakfast that Jesus prepares for his disciples on the beach after a fruitless night trying to fish in the lake after his death. The 'charcoal fire' recalls a similar charcoal fire that Peter warmed his hands by during Jesus' trial, before he denied knowing him (John 18.18 and 21.9). The poem goes into more detail than the Bible does about the fish being grilled: 'carp and catfish' – the hard-edged alliteration with the word 'charcoal' suggests a vivid, clear-edged concrete reality to the succulent food. This is not, as in Luke's narrative, a piece of cold broiled fish, eaten to demonstrate that Jesus' body is real. It is a proper meal for everyone there to enjoy, after working all night. It is not hard to imagine the strident hunger pangs all round: 'This is not hunger, this is resurrection'. Here the poet uses the word 'resurrection' to intensify the concept of human hunger for delicious food, rather than use the existence of hunger to demonstrate the truth of resurrection. It is an exultant word.

The last stanza shows Jesus as a man of strong physical presence – not needy, but in charge, enjoying his food like a healthy young man who is a competent cook. He focuses on the actual taste and texture of the food as it is eaten, the fresh fish with noticeable scales still with the sea's saltiness evident. And then there is the mention of how the salt is felt in the wounds on his hands. This use of a proverb about rubbing salt into wounds functions at several levels. It is a conversational remark, which echoes the informality of the context. But it also throws our attention back to the sufferings of Good Friday. It draws attention to that aspect of the resurrection narratives that concerns Jesus' wounds; when Thomas hears about a resurrection appearance, he refuses to believe until he has seen Jesus himself and touched those wounds – they are a badge of reality which cannot be

denied (John 20.24–29). The resurrection does not undo the suffering and death; the marks of suffering remain on a transformed body,
not a perfect, fantasy one.

The idea in this poem that Jesus himself may have wanted 'to rub
the salt into his wounds' emphasizes that he is so glad to be alive
that he wishes to be reminded of that, not only through his powerful
hunger but by being reminded of his pain by feeling it again. Inevitably, the poem asks us how much we let ourselves be fully present
to our bodily experience, with all its flaws and hurts as well as in the
satisfying of its needs. To be alive to this level of reality might mean
that we also could exclaim, in the presence of great joy, 'This is not
hunger, this is resurrection.'

*Are you glad to be alive? Today, notice and give thanks for the changing
sensations of your body, even its aches and pains.*

Wednesday

The Angel

Sometimes the boulder is rolled away,
but I cannot move it when
I want to. An angel must. Shall
I ever see the angel's face,
or will there always only be
that molten glow outlining every
separate hair and feathered quill,
the sudden wind and odour, sunlight,
music, the pain of my bruised shoulders.

Ruth Fainlight

This brief poem assumes knowledge of the initial resurrection narratives, on the first day of the week after Jesus' crucifixion. Each of the four Gospels contains the story of how some of the women around Jesus (in John it is Mary Magdalene alone) went back to the sepulchre in which his body had been placed to finish the job of anointing and laying out, which had been done very hurriedly as Sabbath fell on the Friday night. What they find is that the boulder that had been rolled across the entrance of the cave-like tomb has been rolled away, and the body has gone. This rather alarming discovery is the first indication that the resurrection has taken place.

Each Gospel mentions the stone explicitly. In Mark's account, the women are discussing, as they approach the place, how they are going to remove it – because it is huge. In Luke's and John's accounts, it has simply gone, or been rolled aside. After they have noticed this, they become aware of a supernatural presence: a young man in white (Mark 16.5); two men in dazzling apparel (Luke 24.4); or two angels in white and then Jesus himself, initially mistaken for the gardener (John 20.14–15). Matthew's story is perhaps the most apocalyptic – as they approach the tomb, there is an earthquake caused by an angel, who descends from heaven and sits on the boulder. 'His appearance was like lightning, and his clothing white as snow' (Matthew 28.2–3).

Fainlight's poem, because of its detailed references to the angel, seems to depend mainly on the narrative in Matthew. The 'boulder' of the Gospel story has become symbolic of something closed and dead within the heart of the believer. Christian reflection has traditionally understood the resurrection to have the power to 'open our graves' in a metaphorical sense (just as in Matthew's Gospel, the graves of the dead are said literally to have opened after Jesus' death).

'Sometimes the boulder is rolled away' – that 'sometimes' marks how the image of the tomb has become a psychic place which the narrator visits regularly, and which is sometimes sealed, sometimes open to light and air. Whatever is the nature of this place, it isn't something that can be made free just by act of will. Just as the women always knew that they were going to find the stone too heavy to shift, the narrator is dependent on divine or at least angelic power to move the rock: 'An angel must.'

The narrator then seeks to describe the angel, and is remarkably successful at conveying both beauty and fearsomeness. Given our culture's penchant for depicting cutesy or sexless beings with unlikely wings and calling them angels, it would be only too easy to end up being bland. She achieves this partly by posing a question, which makes it clear that she has a momentary snatched impression of the angel of the resurrection, but not a direct full-face view. Thus she evokes that deep biblical tradition that it is impossible to look directly at God (or even God's messengers, the angels).

However, she describes some accompanying signs, some of which are about catching, in the corner of the eye, a specific detail ('that molten glow outlining every/ separate hair and feathered quill'), and some of which are general sensory impressions: 'wind and odour, sunlight,/ music'. She also highlights the suddenness of the experience, as if it occurs/appears in a split-second and then is gone. It is like the angelic presence in Charlotte Mew's 'The Call' (p. 24).

But perhaps the most telling detail is the sensation she is left with: 'the pain of my bruised shoulders'. 'Shoulders' echoes the 'boulder' of the first line; we become aware that the narrator has been strenuously pushing at this rock with all the effort she is capable of. The effort has been in vain, because it is the angel and not she herself who has opened the tomb. She has only succeeded in straining herself in a painful way. Yet perhaps making the effort was necessary; certainly, like the women in the Gospel story, if she had not had the courage to visit the tomb, she would certainly have witnessed no angel and experienced no opening of her heart's grave.

Are you ever conscious of being supported by a divine or angelic presence? What do you have to do to put yourself in the way of such help?

Thursday

Resurrection

Easter. The grave clothes of winter
are still here, but the sepulchre
is empty. A messenger
from the tomb tells us
how a stone has been rolled
from the mind, and a tree lightens
the darkness with its blossom.
There are travellers upon the roads
who have heard music blown
from a bare bough, and a child
tells us how the accident
of last year, a machine stranded
beside the way for lack
of petrol is covered with flowers.

R. S. Thomas

This poem, like Ruth Fainlight's 'The Angel', assumes a knowledge of the biblical resurrection narratives, and starts with a detail that only John's Gospel records, namely that when the disciples actually went into the empty tomb, they saw that the body had gone but the grave clothes remained. This is a detail that emphasizes the intervention of a divine power. (Of course, if someone had simply stolen the body, they would hardly have laboriously unwound the bandages and unwrapped the linen head cloth before making off with it.)

Thomas similarly uses the elements of the biblical resurrection narrative to stand for the condition of the individual human heart and its capacity for transformation, but he also weaves in dimensions of the natural world and the wider society. All of creation stands in need of resurrection, and the springtime imagery stands for both the need and the potential for new life and growth.

So 'The grave clothes of winter/ are still here'. There is a point in the northern hemisphere, as spring emerges, when it cannot really be said that winter is fully past, yet everything is on the cusp of a new year's new burgeoning growth. The weather may be bitter, the branches still bare of leaves, the brown and frosted debris of last year's plant growth still much in evidence, not yet overtaken by this year's new green shoots. Yet this is also the moment when some trees put out dramatic blossom.

The next sentence binds together the biblical narrative, the exact point of springtime and the human frame of mind. It speaks of a 'messenger/ from the tomb' – angels were thought of as God's messengers, but in this poem the startling or supernatural qualities of angels are left out; it is a deliberately low-key phrase, as it introduces a series of ordinary 'messengers' who need to be heard also as heralds of the resurrection. And the message is that 'a stone has been rolled/ from the mind' – for Thomas it is often the mind, rather than the heart, that is experienced as carrying a burden or being profoundly blocked or paralysed. This is the site of the believer's struggle in this poem and in several others. In the same sentence, as if it were part of the same transformational process, we hear that 'a tree lightens/ the darkness with its blossom'. There is a beautiful echo of the traditional evening collect which begins, 'Lighten our darkness, O Lord', but it is also a stunning visual evocation of the effect of the early blossom, whose pale blooms stand out sharply against the black branches and the changeable gun-metal skies of early April. At the same time the poet may be evoking the tradition in some churches of decorating at Easter time a cross that has stood stark and empty on Good Friday – this is the 'tree' that lightens our darkness.

There are more messengers. 'Travellers upon the roads' makes us think of the couple who walked to Emmaus and only later realized that the risen Jesus had been walking with them (Luke 24). But they could be contemporary travellers: ordinary people getting about more now that the rural roads are clear of ice, or walkers braving slightly better weather and being rewarded with birdsong ('music blown/ from a bare bough'). But there is a hint that 'travellers' are more than this. It is a term used of gypsies, so you wonder whether the message significantly comes from members of a community who are seen as marginal and whose word may not be believed. Or it could refer to intentional pilgrims, those who are choosing to travel the road of faith and to hear its music.

The final messenger is a child ('whoever does not receive the kingdom of God as a little child will never enter it', Luke 18.17). She (or he) speaks of a local event that is both natural and not quite natural. It isn't uncommon in remote rural places to see the occasional abandoned car that has never quite been rescued from a ditch where an accident left it. It seems that this one has become covered with a blossom – perhaps it went into a blackthorn hedge, one of the earliest trees to come into bloom. This has transformed a wreck into a thing of beauty.

And I suspect that this vehicle and what has happened to it symbolizes the whole environment. It lacks petrol and its progress has been arrested. This will happen to us all when eventually oil and other fossil fuels run out. But the creator will continue to bring resurrection to the whole created world. What humans invent and what humans wreck will continue to be subject to the glory of God.

What for you are the signs of resurrection in our world?

Friday

A Birthday

My heart is like a singing bird
    Whose nest is in a watered shoot:
My heart is like an apple-tree
    Whose boughs are bent with thickset fruit;
My heart is like a rainbow shell
    That paddles in a halcyon sea;
My heart is gladder than all these
    Because my love is come to me.

Raise me a dais of silk and down;
    Hang it with vair and purple dyes;
Carve it in doves and pomegranates,
    And peacocks with a hundred eyes;
Work it in gold and silver grapes,
    In leaves and silver fleur-de-lys;
Because the birthday of my life
    Is come, my love is come to me.

Christina Rossetti

The last two poems in this selected sequence are about joy, about being at home in the love of God for whom we were created and in whom the meaning of our life is held.

This poem by Christina Rossetti is one of the few of hers that seems to be without religious struggle. Although God is not explicitly mentioned, it seems unlikely that this love poem is written for a purely human beloved – there is a solemnity in her celebration, and the focus is upon her own heart rather than on the features or virtues of her lover.

Copious references to the Song of Songs also suggest that this poem is about the human heart in response to God. Whatever may have been the original intention of the erotic biblical poem, there is a rich and compelling Christian tradition which interprets the book as a commentary on the human heart, in love with the overwhelming beauty of the divine, and sensing itself as beautiful and worthy because it is sought and beloved of God. The repeated 'my love is come to me' echoes the Song of Songs, which has passages where the lover comes intimately close, and then seems to draw back. The woman narrator of the Song then goes seeking him around the dark streets, in a desperate and rather shocking fashion (chapter 5). This passionate searching was taken to be a fitting image of the soul seeking God in prayer all night – no earthly considerations of respectability or moderation should get in the way of this life-or-death search. This concept is likely to have appealed to Rossetti (see pp. 35–8 for her approach to prayer as struggle).

The two stanzas dwell first on the external world, and then on the interior. Initially the narrator describes her heart as a 'singing bird', 'an apple-tree', or 'a rainbow shell'. The bird suggests the turtledove in the Song of Songs in a passage famously often used at weddings (2.10–17). The context is that 'the winter is past'; 'the flowers appear', 'the time of singing has come', and the bird's voice is heard in the land as a harbinger of spring and new life. This sense of vigorous new growth is continued in the 'watered shoot' reference, and probably recalls Psalm 1, where the blessed person is the one who bears fruit like a tree 'planted by streams of water' (Psalm 1.3). The apple tree, which is vividly imagined in a brilliant line stuffed with consonants that reflect the weight and volume of the fruit, of course recalls the paradisal tree of life in the garden of Eden. But there are also many references to refreshing apples and apple trees in the garden of the Song of Songs (2.3–5, for example). The 'rainbow shell' is not biblical in itself, but the rainbow is; not only is there iridescent beauty there, but the implicit promise of a new covenant, signified by a rainbow (Genesis 9.8–17).

The second verse builds an equally rich and sumptuous indoor scene of celebration, and here we are put in mind of the artwork of the pre-Raphaelite painters (of whom the poet's brother Dante Gabriel was one). They constructed detailed set-piece scenes with consciously old-fashioned symbolic elements, and stylized, intricately patterned details reminiscent of medieval carvings, and this poem is similar. The 'dais' is a formal platform that would be used as the context for a throne or high table, and the narrator then concentrates on the hangings and decorations to convey the joy of what is to be celebrated there. The vocabulary is ancient: 'vair' means a variegated fur rather like ermine. It is a heraldic term and that is the tone here. 'Purple' again echoes the Song of Songs and its description of the lover, and is the biblical shorthand for rich and authoritative decor (only very high-class people could afford to wear purple, or indeed were allowed to). Doves, pomegranates and grapes are everywhere in the Song of Songs, and I must say, along with the peacock feather eyes, put me in mind of the many William Morris or Liberty print designs that ultimately brought pre-Raphaelite design into many an aspirational living room. But in Rossetti's time this was innovative stuff. The peacock motif may both point to the resurrection (peacocks are traditional symbols of it) and also evoke the exotic materials and furniture that were being imported during Rossetti's time.

The sense of newness and delight is there in the 'birthday of my life' – surely a sort of resurrection experience in the spiritual life; and in the imperative mood of the second verse – 'Raise me a dais', 'Hang it', 'Carve it', 'Work it' – there is the sense not only of a lifted heart but a new authority in the believer, and a willingness to be celebrated herself, and unapologetically to exult in that.

In your relationship with God, what do you exult in?

Saturday

And that will be heaven

and that will be heaven

and that will be heaven
at last   the first unclouded
seeing

   to stand like the sunflower
turned full face to the sun   drenched
with light   in the still centre
held   while the circling planets
hum with an utter joy

     seeing and knowing
at last   in every particle
seen and known   and not turning
away

   never turning away
again

Evangeline Paterson

This book began Lent with a poem that started with turning aside
to glance at a bright sunlit field and ended with contemplating 'the
eternity that awaits you'. The sequence ends with a poem that seeks
to gaze directly at the expectation of heaven.

The poem begins and ends as if in the middle of a sentence. Ordinary punctuation is absent; there are just pauses and the turning
of lines, but the pace is slow rather than exuberant. No sentence is
actually completed; it is as if the narrator is caught up in something

where it is not possible, or not necessary, to finish sentences. There are things that cannot be said in a final way, and this doesn't matter. Inarticulacy is the point.

'That will be heaven' is a common enough exaggeration we use to express satisfaction with an arrangement that looks as if it will work well for us. Here the phrase is repeated after a line gap, as if to underline that a quite different view of what is genuinely 'heaven' is in order. The tone is not severe or critical; it is just taking us down several levels of depth.

'At last' – rather like the Rossetti poem, this is a stage, it is implied, that is reached after a lifetime of earnest searching. The 'first unclouded/ seeing' and the later 'in every particle/ seen and known' remind us of the great hymn to love: 'For now we see in a mirror dimly, but then we will see face to face. Now I know only in part; then I will know fully, even as I have been fully known' (1 Corinthians 13.12). The passage in 2 Corinthians 3.14–18 about veiled and unveiled faces may also be present behind the poem.

Within this biblical mysticism the poem offers the image of the 'sunflower/ turned full face to the sun'. The French word for the flower, *tournesol*, explicitly highlights what this dramatic plant actually does during the day when it is in bloom: it literally turns around to present its face to wherever the sun is in the sky. At the same time, the sun-like shape of the flower head makes it seem as if the sunflower has taken on the very countenance of the thing it lives by and seems to worship. The turning of the sunflower by day is mirrored in the galaxies with the circling of the planets in the night sky, around the sun which is the centre of their gravitational path and the reason why they exist and move at all.

Throughout our lives, we inevitably go through a pattern of being distracted and turning away from God and then consciously, as in Lent, turning aside to try to approach and gaze at God once more. As we have seen, to gaze directly is not given to us in this life. The poet here imagines heaven as the place where that is no longer impossible. May it be true.

Spend time in silence, with your heart turned 'full face to the sun'.

Acknowledgements

Nicholas Albery, 'To Know A Poem By Heart', *A Poem for the Day 2*, Chatto and Windus, 2003. Reproduced by permission of Josefine Speyer of the Natural Death Centre.

Margaret Atwood, 'It is dangerous to read newspapers' and 'The Moment', in *Eating Fire: Selected Poetry 1965–1995*, Virago, 1998. Reproduced with permission of Curtis Brown Group Ltd, London, on behalf of Margaret Atwood. Copyright © Margaret Atwood 1995.

Maria Boulding (translator), Augustine, *Confessions* X.27.38, New City Press, 1997. Used by permission of the Augustinian Heritage Institute.

Charles Causley, 'I am the great sun', *Collected Poems*, Macmillan, 1992. Used by permission of David Higham Associates Ltd.

E. E. Cummings, 'i am a little church(no great cathedral)', and 'i thank You God for most this amazing' are reprinted from *Complete Poems 1904–1962*, by E. E. Cummings, edited by George J. Firmage, by permission of W. W. Norton & Company, Inc. Copyright © 1991 by the Trustees for the E. E. Cummings Trust and George James Firmage.

Carol Ann Duffy, 'Homesick' is taken from *Selling Manhattan* by Carol Ann Duffy, published by Anvil Press in 1987.

Ruth Fainlight, 'The Angel', *New and Collected Poems*, Bloodaxe Books, 2010. Used by permission of the author.

U. A. Fanthorpe, 'Friends' Meeting House, Frenchay, Bristol', *New and Collected Poems*, Enitharmon Press, 2010. Copyright R. V. Bailey. 'Afterwards', *Consequences*, Peterloo Poets, 2000. Copyright R. V. Bailey.

Robert Frost, 'Fire and Ice', *The Poetry of Robert Frost*, edited by Edward Connery Lathem, published by Jonathan Cape. Reprinted by permission of the Random House Group Ltd.

Acknowledgements

Kerry Hardie, 'Sheep Fair Day', *The Sky Didn't Fall*, Gallery Press, 2003, by kind permission of the author and The Gallery Press, Loughcrew, Oldcastle, County Meath, Ireland.

Robert Hayden, 'Those Winter Sundays', copyright © 1966 by Robert Hayden, from *Collected Poems of Robert Hayden*, by Robert Hayden, edited by Frederick Glaysher. Used by permission of Liveright Publishing Corporation.

Seamus Heaney, 'The Skylight', from 'Glanmore Revisited (7)', *Opened Ground: Poems 1966–1996*, Faber and Faber Ltd, 1998.

Elizabeth Jennings, 'Rembrandt's Late Self-Portraits', *New Collected Poems*, Carcanet Press Ltd, 2002. Used by permission of David Higham Associates Ltd.

Philip Larkin, 'The Trees', *Collected Poems*, Faber and Faber Ltd, 1988.

Denise Levertov, 'On a Theme by Thomas Merton', *A Door in the Hive/Evening Train*, p. 205, Bloodaxe Books, 1993. 'Ikon: The Harrowing of Hell', in Paul A. Lacey (ed.), *New Selected Poetry*, Bloodaxe Books, 2003. Reproduced by permission of Pollinger Limited and New Directions.

Roger McGough, 'The Wrong Beds', in *The Collected Poems*, Viking, 2003. Used by permission of the author.

Kei Miller, 'Speaking in tongues', in *There is an Anger that Moves*, Carcanet Press Ltd, 2007.

Evangeline Paterson, 'And that will be heaven', in Mary Batchelor (ed.), *The Lion Book of Christian Poetry*, Lion, 2005.

Adrienne Rich, 'The problem', Poem 18 of 'Contradictions: Tracking Poems'. Copyright © 2002, 1986 by Adrienne Rich, from *The Fact of a Doorframe: Selected Poems 1950–2001* by Adrienne Rich. Used by permission of the author and W. W. Norton & Company, Inc.

Michael Symmons Roberts, 'Food for risen bodies – II', *Corpus*, Jonathan Cape, 2004. Used by permission of the author.

E. J. Scovell, 'Deaths of Flowers', in *Selected Poems of E. J. Scovell*, Carcanet Press Ltd, 1991.

Acknowledgements

R. S. Thomas, 'The Bright Field', *Laboratories of the Spirit*, Macmillan, 1975. 'The Kingdom', *H'm*, Macmillan, 1972. 'Resurrection', *Selected Poems*, Penguin Books, London, 2003 © Kunjana Thomas 2001.

Jean M. Watt, 'Lent', in Jenny Robertson (ed.), *A Touch of Flame: An Anthology of Contemporary Christian Poetry*, Lion, 1989.

Rowan Williams, 'I Saw him Standing' (translation from the Welsh of Ann Griffiths' 'Yr Arglwydd Iesu'), and 'Rublev', both from *The Poems of Rowan Williams*, reprinted by permission of the author and the publisher, The Perpetua Press, 2002.

All biblical quotations are taken from the New Revised Standard Version of the Bible, copyright © 1989 by the Division of Christian Education of the National Council of the Churches of Christ in the USA. Used by permission. All rights reserved.

'Remember that you are dust' (p. 6) is from the Liturgy of Ash Wednesday, *Common Worship: Times and Seasons*, copyright © The Archbishops' Council, 2006, and is reproduced by permission. <copyright@c-of-e.org.uk>

'Earth to earth' (p. 6) is from the Funeral Service, *Common Worship: Pastoral Services*, copyright © The Archbishops' Council, 2005, and is reproduced by permission. <copyright@c-of-e.org.uk>

Every effort has been made to trace copyright holders and make correct acknowledgements. Please contact the publisher regarding any omission or inaccuracy.

My grateful thanks are due to Dr Jill Robson and Nicky Woods, who commented on my draft. Any remaining errors or inaccuracies are of course my own.